Mastering the ZX SPECTRUM

ELLIS HORWOOD BOOKS IN COMPUTING

MASTERING THE COMMODORE 64
A.J. JONES, Brunel University, and G. CARPENTER, Racal Tacticom Ltd.

STRUCTURED PROGRAMMING WITH BBC BASIC
ROY ATHERTON, Bulmershe College, Reading

MASTERING THE VIC-20
A.J. JONES, Brunel University, E.A. COLEY, Maystar Microcomputers Ltd. Wokingham, and D.G.J. COLE, British Aerospace, Bracknell

BEGINNING micro-PROLOG 2nd Revised Edition
RICHARD ENNALS, University of London

GETTING STARTED ON THE ORIC-1
D.G.J. COLE, British Aerospace, Bracknell

BEGINNING COMAL
BORGE CHRISTENSEN, Tonder College of Higher Education, Tonder, Denmark

WINNING GAMES ON THE COMMODORE 64
TERRY BARRETT, Freelance Programmer, and STEPHEN COLWILL, Sandhurst School, Surrey

LOGO: A GUIDE TO LEARNING THROUGH PROGRAMMING
PETER GOODYEAR, Avery Hill College, London

WINNING GAMES ON THE VIC-20
TERRY BARRETT, Freelance Programmer, and A.J. JONES, Brunel University

MASTERING THE ACORN ELECTRON
SIMON and JOHN MATTHEWS, University of Exeter

MASTERING THE ZX SPECTRUM
LAWRIE MOORE, freelance writer and lecturer, formerly University of London

BEGINNING LISP
AJIT NARAYANAN, Exeter University

Mastering the ZX SPECTRUM

Lawrie Moore

ELLIS HORWOOD LIMITED
Publishers · Chichester

JOHN WILEY & SONS INC
New York · Chichester · Brisbane · Toronto · Singapore

First published in 1983 by
ELLIS HORWOOD LIMITED
Market Cross House, Cooper Street, Chichester,
West Sussex PO19 1EB, England

Distributors:

Australia, New Zealand, South-east Asia:
Jacaranda-Wiley Ltd., Jacaranda Press
JOHN WILEY & SONS INC.
GPO Box 859, Brisbane, Queensland 4001, Australia

Canada:
JOHN WILEY & SONS CANADA LIMITED
22 Worcester Road, Rexdale, Ontario, Canada

Europe, Africa:
JOHN WILEY & SONS LIMITED
Baffins Lane, Chichester, West Sussex, England

North and South America and the rest of the world:
JOHN WILEY & SONS INC.
605 Third Avenue, New York, NY 10158, USA

British Library Cataloguing in Publication Data
Moore, Lawrie
Mastering the ZX Spectrum. –
(Ellis Horwood books in computing)
1. Sinclair ZX Spectrum (Computer)
I. Title
001.64'04 QA76.8.S625

ISBN 0-85312-700-X (Ellis Horwood Limited)

Typeset by Ellis Horwood Ltd.
Printed in Great Britain by R. J. Acford, Chichester.

Contents

Introductory digression

The problem is:

How do you tell what
this book is like without
reading it?

Method 1:

Flip through the pages with your thumb
one at a time,
very rapidly,
at eye level,
and see
whether it reminds you of
a good film.

Method 2:

Stick a pin in the bookseller,
and don't stop,
until he tells you
all about the book.

Method 3:

Read what the author says at the beginning
(like right here?).
This is a terrible method –
nearly as bad as reading
the book itself.

Take this book. You might never realize until you've bought it and read it, how good it is. So, to make life easier for you, here is some straight information about this book.

It teaches you the basic IDEAS behind the technique of programming, so that you know what you are doing.

These days, everyone is so busy telling you *what* to do and *never mind why*, that you can easily get pushed into working at something without knowing what you are doing.

If you want to learn to program, you can't just program nothing, there has to be some worthwhile problem to solve. Now there is a funny thing about solving problems. Sometimes, the only reason you tackle a problem is because you *need* the *solution*. But that's no real fun. The real fun is when what you really want is *not* the answer but the fun of *finding it*. That's what programming is all about.

In this book a lot of the programming is about how to produce pretty patterns on the screen. Some is about text processing, and a lot *seems* to be about producing music from your computer. But it isn't really just about those things at all, because all the tricks and techniques and know-how that are explained are the basic methods you need to understand for *all* programming.

Not just for programming in BASIC.
Not just for programming the Sinclair ZX Spectrum.
Not just for writing one particular kind of program.

This book uses a number of smallish programs as mini-projects to illustrate how to use the computer to implement a particular programming method. But then all these programs are linked together as subroutines in a large project which produces a challenging and fascinating game called the MUSIC PROGRAM. In order to do this, you need to learn how to design a (large) program, which is quite a different problem from writing a lot of small ones. Most programming books don't teach you anything about that – they leave you to muddle through or get stuck.

If you don't want to learn programming AND ENJOY IT –

If you don't want to learn programming AND KNOW WHAT YOU'RE DOING –

If you want to miss the fun of playing this *entirely different* computer game called the MUSIC PROGRAM –

Then this book is not for you.

BUT:

Lifetime Guarantee
The author personally guarantees that he will refund your money, in person, if you haven't learned to program to a standard which is to his satisfaction, before the end of his lifetime. (Offer closes on the author's fourteenth birthday.)

* * * * * *

If you still don't know what this book is like – and you still want to know – you'll just have to read it.

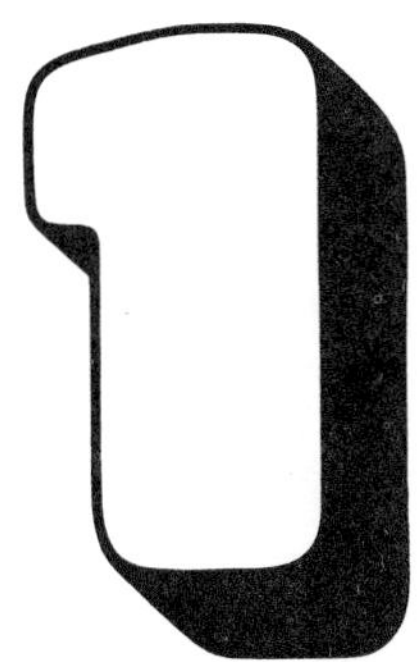

Keys to success

There are already many books on programming the Sinclair ZX Spectrum Computer. This one is different because it assumes you are a beginner, and do not already know what all the buzz-words mean.

It also assumes you don't know how to go about writing programs for yourself. It is not good enough merely to be told the rules, nor to have a mass of information thrown at you, giving you mental indigestion.

Programming is not a black art, even though the results might sometimes fill us with wonder. It can be learned with a little effort by anyone, provided they are shown the steps to take, one at a time, and actually try them out before going on to the next one.

Programming is a bit like swimming. You can't learn to swim just from a book. You have to get into the water. But it is easier than swimming because you can stop at any point of difficulty and pick up this book, without drowning!

Some people learn to program by just trying anything they think of until they find something that works. This is one of the worst ways of learning, because everything is always a muddle, even when you muddle your way through. Imagine learning to fly an airplane or drive a car that way! As I said before, programming is safer than swimming. It is certainly safer than flying, or driving a car.

But it can be more exciting, thrilling, rewarding and satisfying than any of these, in a way which gives you the feeling that you have just created an elegant picture, a piece of music, or a poem. The main virtue of well-written programs is simplicity not complexity. That is what makes them satisfying, and that is what makes it easy to learn to program well, provided you are given the right kind of help, the kind of help that helps you to learn for yourself, and to understand what you are doing.

What can the computer do?

Basically the computer can do four things:

It can PRINT information.
It can STORE the information you give it.
It can SELECT from that information the piece or pieces you want.
It can RE-ARRANGE or CHANGE it in some systematic way.

So connect up your computer and switch it on. Make yourself comfortable with the keyboard within reach and let's get started. When you learn to drive a car, the first thing you need is to learn where the controls are located. The computer has a whole keyboard of controls, so it is even more important to become familiar with them, and this is what we'll do right now.

The very first thing to realize is that you have to be able to find the keys you want on the keyboard. Each key has quite a number of markings, but the main ones are the letters of the alphabet, and these are arranged in a strange order called the 'standard typewriter keyboard'. Until you have become familiar with it, this ensures that you will be unable to find the key you want.

But we have ways of making you type! Let us take a critical look at this lovable monster. Actually there are only four rows of keys. The top row is a cinch – just the digits 1 to 9 arranged in order, followed by zero (written Ø to distinguish it from the letter O, which means something entirely different, and is stored inside the computer in a way that looks nothing like zero).

The second row is arranged in a QWERTY UI OP manner (pronouced QWERTY EWY OP).

The phrase querty ui op may be unfamiliar to you, but it is a useful one which you should get to know, because it describes the second row absolutely perfectly. It rolls off the tongue pleasantly with a little practice. Saying it over to yourself aloud a few times while you are looking for a letter can be QWERTY UIsful OPeration.

The third row is psychologically interesting because it throws light on the mind of the man who designed the 'standard typewriter keyboard'. This row is the first half of the alphabet in correct alphabetic order. Well nearly. It starts off with A, S. Of course, its true that S isn't in the first half, and A is the only vowel included. But the rest of the row runs from D to L through the alphabet, excluding vowels.

There is only one row left, the bottom row. This row was brought into the design because there were some letters left over. By this time, the problem of designing the standard keyboard had beaten the designer into a state of nervous exhaustion, but he showed absolutely incredible foresight by starting this row with the first name of our computer – ZX. All that remains to be remembered is CV and then BNM. Now CV stands for a well-known Latin phrase which most people have never met, and personally I have no trouble at all in remembering BNM because these are the registration letters on my car.

Getting to know the standard keyboard is a useful start, but the Sinclair ZX keyboard is way ahead of the standard keyboard as a piece of design. The idea is to save you a lot of typing. There are a number of words the computer has been taught to recognize, words you will need to use all the time. These words are called KEYWORDS. Each of them is keyed into the computer by depressing a single key, not – repeat NOT – by spelling it out on the keyboard. But to make this possible without introducing a large number of extra keys, nearly every key has to be capable of meaning four or even five different things! Even on the simple-minded old standard typewriter keyboard each key may mean two different things, like a letter in small type (called lower-case) or the same letter in capitals (called upper-case). Changing from one set of meanings to another on the keyboard is called changing shift.

Altogether there are 242 different meanings, any one of which you can convey to the computer by just a single key depression, provided the keyboard is in the correct shift for the meaning required. Instead of only two shifts the Spectrum has five, and they are generally called MODES. Each of the 242 different meanings is denoted by a Spectrum CHARACTER. Thus a character may be a single symbol, such as a lower-case letter, an upper-case letter, a digit, a square or round bracket, a plus-symbol, an equals symbol, an asterisk, and so on. A character may also be a compound token such as a KEYWORD. Another word for Spectrum character is the word TOKEN.

Side A of the Psion Horizon cassette which comes free with the Spectrum contains an excellent program that teaches you to understand and become familiar with the way the Spectrum keyboard works. It turns what could be a chore into a fun game. Run through this tape once or twice until you are throughly at ease using the Spectrum keyboard. Do it now.

First of all, you will find that if you hold a key down, whatever token you get is repeated for as long as you hold the key down. Secondly, to delete any token you have just entered, you depress CAPS-SHIFT *and* DELETE both at the same time. You can see both of these operations working by holding down for a line of tokens, and then holding down to delete them.

When you depress a key, the token you get depends on two things. The first and most obvious is which key you hit. The second is the keyboard MODE. There are five modes, and the current mode is shown on the screen by the flashing character in a black box. This is the CURSOR.

(Anything you enter is displayed on the screen at the position shown by the cursor.) Each mode is indicated by its initial letter, and the five modes are:

Keyword mode	–	for the special word shown in white on the key.
Letter mode	–	for an individual (lower-case) letter.
Capitals mode	–	for an individual (upper-case) letter.
Extended mode	–	for the token shown in red or green ABOVE or BELOW the key.
Graphics mode	–	for the patterns shown in white on keys 1 to 8.

The Spectrum handbook gives a good short description of the way the keyboard works, and the Psion Horizon cassette cannot be beaten as a tutor. But above all, you do need to understand the ideas behind the way the keyboard switches from mode to mode.

[K] mode is different from the others (KEYWORDS):

The computer knows when you need to be in [K] mode; *and* when you *don't* need it. So, being an 'intelligent' system, it puts you into or out of [K] mode as required. (It always thinks it knows best!)

You always need [K] mode at the beginning of an instruction. While in [K] mode you can enter either a keyword, or a line-number followed by a keyword, and once you have done that, the computer automatically switches you into [L] mode, which is the 'normal' mode which you need most of the time.

A useful way to think of it is that [L] mode (Letter-mode) is the normal mode. And there are two push-button type ON/OFF switches which work just like the push-button switch on a bedside lamp. There is a separate push-button for each of the two modes:

CAPS MODE
GRAPHICS MODE

To get into [C] mode (CAPS):
you press CAPS-SHIFT *and* CAPS-LOCK *both at the same time.*
To get back out of it you do the same thing again!
To get into [G] mode (GRAPHICS):
you press CAPS-SHIFT *and* GRAPHICS *both at the same time.*
To get back out of it you do the same thing again!

'Both at the same time!'

You should realize that the computer understands the English language in a rather pedantic (and irritating) way. 'Both at the same time' is a very dangerous phrase.

When you want the computer to understand that you have pushed a shift key and some other key 'both at the same time', it is essential that, actually, you press the shift key *first,* and hold it down while you press the other key.

The reason for this is quite straightforward. If you try to press two keys simultaneously, one of them is *certain to make contact before the other* (*by at least a* few millionths of a second). If it is the shift key that makes contact first, thats OK, but otherwise, as they say, you are in schtuhk!

Whenever you 'get back out' of [C] or [G] , you find yourself in the same mode you were in before. All you have to remember is

(i) Look at the Cursor on the screen to see what mode you are in *before* you change mode.
(ii) Look at the Cursor on the screen to see what mode you are in *after* you change mode.

E mode is even more special and different (EXTENDED):

To get into E mode

you press CAPS-SHIFT *and* SYMBOL-SHIFT *both at the same time*

But E mode is partly switched by you, and partly automatic. You have to switch into it.

But as soon as you press an Extended Token-Symbol the computer automatically switches you back out again, because you don't usually need it for more than one token at a time.

If you get into a mess (through accidentally pressing the wrong keys), the golden rule is:

(i) Look at the cursor on the screen to see which mode you are in.
(ii) Change mode if required, and then look again to check.

Using extended mode

You need extended mode to enter the tokens printed ABOVE the bottom three rows of keys (in green), or BELOW all four rows of keys (in red).

So *first*

Press CAPS-SHIFT *and* SYMBOL SHIFT

This gives you immediate access to the token ABOVE each key, printed in GREEN.

If you want the RED token, printed BELOW, provided you are already in E mode, then

press the key required while holding SYMBOL-SHIFT down.

Examples

(1) Assuming you are in L mode; to enter the INT token
 (i) Change mode to E by pressing CAPS-SHIFT *and* SYMBOL-SHIFT both at the same time.
 (ii) Press INT (printed in GREEN above the R key).
(2) Assuming you are in L mode; to enter VERIFY
 (i) Change mode to E by pressing CAPS-SHIFT *and* SYMBOL-SHIFT both at the same time.
 (ii) Press SYMBOL-SHIFT *and* VERIFY both at the same time. (VERIFY is printed in RED below the R key).

Using graphics mode

You need graphics mode to enter the mosaic cubist shapes shown in black-and-white on the top row of the keyboard. So first:

press CAPS-SHIFT *and* GRAHICS *'both at the same time'*

(GRAPHICS is printed in WHITE above key 9). This gives you immediate access to the eight graphics symbols shown on keys 1 to 8.

In each case, if you press any one of these eight keys alone, you get the symbol shown. But if you press it together with CAPS-SHIFT, you get its 'inverse'. That means that the black and white of the symbol are reversed.

Examples

(1) key 1 alone gives

key 1 with CAPS-SHIFT gives

(2) key 6 alone gives

key 6 with CAPS-SHIFT gives

Keyboard practice
It is essential to get a little practice with the keyboard by trying out for yourself all the operations described, until you have seen for yourself how the keyboard works, and shown that you are the boss, not it!

Loading your first cassette
'Loading' from cassette means copying the information on the cassette into computer memory.

'Saving' is the opposite – copying information from computer memory onto a cassette.

To load a program on cassette, you enter

LOAD "program-name"

where program-name is a string of characters used to name the program when it was SAVEd.

If the program you want to LOAD is the next program on the tape you can leave out the name, and simply enter

LOAD " "

You will see the command displayed at the bottom of the screen as you type it in. But as soon as you press ENTER, the screen goes blank.

Always ensure before you start that the tape is fully rewound, or the LOAD might not work.

Sometimes people have trouble with their first LOAD, and if they don't know exactly what should happen, it can be very frustrating.

When you start the cassette playing, the border of the screen will change colour about once a second until some information is found on the tape. Then the border changes to horizontal coloured stripes about the width of a line of characters. The coloured stripes (blue and red) move slowly up the screen and there is a steady high-pitched whine. After a few seconds the bands disappear briefly, and on the screen appears the message:

program :

except that on the right of the colon the program name will be displayed in addition. At this instant there is a glitch in the sound, and new coloured horizontal bands appear in the border, narrower and more jagged than before. The sound also becomes more jagged. This continues until the end of information is reached, when usually (but not always) a message is displayed at the bottom of the screen

Ø OK, Ø:1

which, of course, is the computer's friendly way of reassuring you. At this point you can stop the tape, knowing that all is well.

However, you may get the message

Tape loading error

The usual cause of this when first trying to LOAD is that the volume control on the tape recorder needs adjusting. Don't adjust it WHILE you are loading, but try it at various levels until you load successfully. Then stick a piece of sticky tape over it so that it doesn't get accidentally moved.

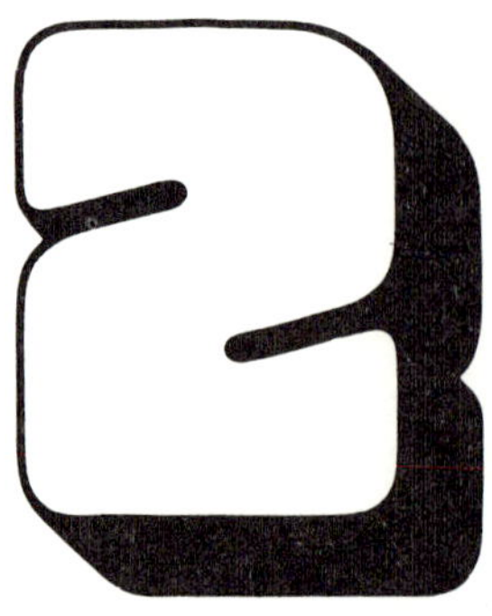

Getting information in and displaying it

The easiest way of getting information into the computer is to type it in using the keyboard. Every time you press a key, one TOKEN of data is entered. Although there are different kinds of token, for example letters, digits, keywords, the computer stores each one of them in exactly the same way, using what is called a BYTE of its memory for each token. One byte of memory holds a sequence of electromagnetic impulses which can be re-arranged into just exactly 256 different and distinct patterns, each of which is assigned an integer code value in the range 0 to 255. Thus each token that can be entered into the computer store has an integer code value from 0 to 255. Appendix 4 gives these in alphabetic order of characters or token-names.

All this stuff inside the computer is called DATA, and it goes into the computer one byte at a time. Here is a sample selection of these TOKENS and their CODE-VALUES:

Code Value	Token	Code Value	Token	Code Value	Token
50	"2"	100	"d"	135	"[illegible]"
51	"3"	101	"e"	136	"[illegible]"
52	"4"	102	"f"	137	"[illegible]"
53	"5"	103	"g"	138	"[illegible]"
54	"6"	104	"h"	139	"[illegible]"
55	"7"	105	"i"	140	"[illegible]"
56	"8"	106	"j"	141	"[illegible]"
57	"9"	107	"k"	142	"[illegible]"
58	":"	108	"l"	143	"[illegible]"
59	";"	109	"m"	144	"A"
60	"<"	110	"n"	145	"B"

You can see that all the stuff you can get into the computer from the keyboard is made up of these TOKENS. Some of them are digits. Some are letters. Some are keywords. Some are graphic symbols. As far as the computer is concerned, each one is stored in the same way. Every token has a code-value, and what the computer stores is the code-value.

As you can see from the table, even the digits have code-values, and the code-value of a digit has nothing to do with the numerical value it represents if you think of it as a number. Both you and the computer can tell whether it is a token or a number quite easily. If it is inside quote-marks (as in the table above) then it is a token. If not, then it is a number. The computer stores *numbers* in quite a different way from tokens, and it has ways of recognizing whether to treat things in store as numbers or tokens. It has its own built-in internal programs for recognizing numeric values and for doing arithmetic with them.

When you store an integer in the computer, you tell it whether to store the integer as a numeric value, or as a string of characters (digit-tokens) by using quote-marks. Sometimes, but not often, it doesn't matter whether the computer stores numbers or tokens. For example, if you ENTER

PRINT 123

this a direct instruction which is obeyed immediately, and the computer will display on the screen the number

123

and if instead you ENTER

PRINT "123"

the computer will display on the screen exactly the same

123

However, if you try

PRINT 123+456

and then try

PRINT "123"+"456"

there is a spectacular difference.

The expression 123+456 tells the computer to store 123 and 456 as numeric values, not strings of characters. Because they are numeric values, the computer takes the plus symbol between them to mean arithmetic addition, hence the result which it prints is their sum, 579.

But the expression "123"+"456" has quote-marks round each of the two values, and therefore the computer stores each of them as three characters, i.e. as a character-string. Because they are character-values, not numeric values, the computer takes the plus symbol to mean glueing the two strings together, not arithmetic addition, and therefore prints 123456. Yet another variation of this instruction, by placing quote-marks in a different position, is

PRINT "123+456"

This time there is just a single string of characters to print. Everthing inside quote-marks is just characters, and the computer does not interpret it to mean anything at all. That is why, this time, the plus is not interpreted to mean arithmetic addition, glueing-together strings, or anything else. It is just one of the seven characters inside the quote marks, and is treated no differently from the others. The whole string is merely displayed on the screen.

By the time you have reached this point, you should already have got out your computer, switched it on, and tried out this use of quote-marks. If not, then do it now. Then try a little experimenting with your own examples. The best and most enjoyable way to learn to master your computer is to combine reading this book with trying out and doing the things being described and discussed. So every time you settle down to read a bit more of the book, make sure your computer is already switched on and at your fingertips.

Storing information and naming it

Sometimes you want to store items of data and get the computer to do something more complex with them than just print them out. In any case, you can always give each item of data a name as well as a value. The name you choose to give it has to follow a few simple rules, depending on the type of value you want stored. For a number value you can choose any name, like 'jane', or 'stephen', or 'matthew'. It has to begin with a letter, but it may contain digits or even spaces as well as letters. For example, 'simple simon', or 'Elizabeth 2nd' are both perfectly acceptable to the computer as names for *number* values.

For a data item which is not numeric, the rules for choosing the name are different. The name must consist of a single letter followed immediately by the dollar symbol, such as 'x$', or 'X$', or 'z$' or 'A$'. All names of character-type data items have to end with '$'.

So there are two kinds of names for items of data which are stored in the computer. Some end in a $ sign and some don't. A name that ends in a dollar-sign can be used ONLY for a token (or a string of tokens). To name a data-item, you can use the LET instruction. For example

```
LET x$ = "do you come here often ?"
```

gives the name, x$ to the string of tokens inside the quote marks. In this example, the string contains 24 tokens. Try counting them and see if you agree that there are 24. This total doesn't include the quotemarks, but it does include every token inside them, including the spaces between words.

When you see a name like x$, or y$ or a$, you *know* it is the name of a string of tokens (possibly just one token), and cannot possibly be the name of a data item which is a number. On the other hand, you can write

```
LET x = 23
```

or

```
LET greedy = 842
```

and when you see any name which *doesn't end in a dollar-sign, you know* that its value is a *number* and *not* a string of tokens.

So the type of value stored by the computer is reflected in the type of name that is allowed for it. Names ending in dollar-signs are for strings, and names without dollar-signs are for numbers.

But note that the computer does not distinguish between capital letters and lower-case letters when they occur in names. So far as the computer is concerned the names:

xyz and XYZ are the same:
x$ and X$ are the same

As well as storing items of data, the computer can store the instructions you give it. When you enter the instruction

```
PRINT "Hello there"
```

the computer obeys the instruction, but does not store it, so if you want the same instruction obeyed more than once you must type it in every single time you want it obeyed. However, you can get the computer to store any instruction if you wish, merely by giving it a name. The computer is very fussy about the names you give to instructions. Unlike data items they cannot contain any letters at all, but instead they must be integer numbers in the range from 1 to 9999.

Let us now try giving names to some data items and to some instructions. Try entering

```
500  PRINT "Hello there – glad to know you"
```

The computer displays the instruction, but doesn't carry it out. But if you now enter

```
RUN 500
```

the computer will obey the instruction named '500'.

Now enter

```
500  LET age = 998
515  LET N$ = "METHUSELA"
530  LET P$ = " is my name. "
545  LET Q$ = " is my age."
560  PRINT N$;P$;age;Q$
```

The first line is a new instruction called '500', and as a result the old one, which was originally called '500' is now lost, or overwritten by the new one with the same name. If and when this instruction is obeyed, but not before, then the numeric value, 998, will be stored, and given the name 'age'.

The second line is a new instruction with a new name, '515'. This name is different from any previously existing name, so this instruction is stored without any previous instruction being lost. Again, it is important to note and understand that the instruction is not yet obeyed, merely stored.

The third and fourth lines have similar effects. They result in the storage of two more instructions. In each case the instruction itself is not yet obeyed, merely stored. If and when these four instructions do get obeyed, then what happens is that the data items they contain are themselves stored and named.

The fifth line again stores an instruction without obeying it; but this instruction is rather different from the others: it is a PRINT instruction. When it comes to be obeyed, the computer will display in turn upon the screen each of the data items whose names appear in the list of names, separated by semicolons, which follows the keyword PRINT.

Whenever you want these instructions obeyed, you just enter the instruction

```
RUN 500
```

The instruction RUN 500 does not itself have a name, so it is not stored, only obeyed. 'RUN 500' tells the computer to obey the instruction which is named 500. The name of an instruction is usually called its line-number. Because line 500 is followed by four other stored instructions, each of these is obeyed in sequence, one after the other in turn, and you will see the result displayed upon the screen. If you enter RUN, without naming an instruction, the computer will start obeying the instruction with the lowest line-number it has stored. It will then carry on to the next lowest line-number, and so on, in turn, until there are no more stored instructions left. Any sequence of stored instructions which are to be obeyed one after the other like this is called a program. That's what a program is!

Oh dear – it didn't work!

Hopefully, when you typed in the Methusela program, it did work. But as it may be one of the very first programs you have typed in, it just may have happened that it *didn't* work. Life is like that. If something can go wrong, it usually does!

So don't be down-hearted. One of the first things you learn with computers is that they are too stupid to read your mind or catch on to what you are trying to do. People, of course, are quite different. They are not stupid. They actch on pretty easily to what you are trying to do, even though you may not have said so very clearly or correctly. (Did you 'actch on'?).

With the computer, you only need to make a trivial slip and type in something almost the same (but not quite) as you intended, and the computer gets it wrong!

So if your program didn't work, look very carefully at it and compare it character by character (*NOT* word by word) with what you copied from. You will probably spot a small difference. But you must not *read* what you are comparing! If you do, your mind's eye will automatically convert what you see to what you think *should* be there. It is better to pretend you can't read, and look at each token separately (including spaces) to see what the computer thinks is there. As a last resort, try typing it in again, from scratch.

Possibly the computer refused to accept the line you tried to ENTER. If so, when you pressed ENTER, an additional character appeared in the line you were trying to enter – a flashing question-mark, that is '?'. This appears either immediately before or immediately after the token the computer doesn't like. This is helpful because you know that the mistake was made somewhere before there and not later in the line. But it may not be at the point where the '?' is flashing. It may be much earlier in the line. The computer looks at each token in turn, and if what it reads is legal so far then it carries on reading the line. So long as it finds something acceptable, it will carry on.

If you get puzzled about what is wrong in this sort of situation, it is necessary to go back to the user manual and consult the rules about what is allowed and what isn't. Chapter 8 deals in more detail with trouble-shooting. But meanwhile let's return to the Methusela program.

More about using PRINT

Line 560 above had four items to print, separated by semicolons.

You can have as many items as you like in the list in a PRINT instruction, but they must be separated by one of three kinds of separator. You can mix the separators in the same list just how you like. The separators you can use are

SEMICOLON	i.e. ";"	(Symbol-Shift, o)
COMMA	i.e. ","	(Symbol-Shift, n)
APOSTROPHE	i.e. "'"	(Symbol-Shift, 7)

and each has a different effect on where the next item gets displayed:

SEMICOLON	all squashed up as close as possible
APOSTROPHE	start a new line
COMMA	leaves at least one space and then starts in column 17 or a new line, whichever comes first. (Column 17 is half-way across the screen.)

Try changing the separators in line 560, first to commas, then to apostrophes, and you will see the effect.

You can if you like put comma or semicolon at the *end* of a PRINT statement, after the last item. Nothing at all at the end is the same as apostrophe – the next PRINT statement begins on a new line. To see the effect of putting separators at the end, repeat line 560 with a new line number 570, so that there are now two PRINT instructions stored.

If you want one or more blank lines, you can insert extra apostrophes. Each one gives another new line.

```
PRINT "line 1" ' ' ' "line 2"
```

will leave *two blank lines* between 'line 1' and 'line 2'.

```
100  PRINT "line 1"
110  PRINT
120  PRINT
130  PRINT "line 2"
```

does the same, because PRINT by itself simply gives a new line. Each separate PRINT statement starts a new line unless the previous one to be obeyed ended in " ; " or " , ". Try all the combinations until you can see how it works.

Incidentally, if you entered lines 100 to 130 above, and then entered RUN, you will have noticed that, of course, after completing line 130, the computer went on and obeyed lines 500 to 560, which you stored previously. To stop this happening, you can enter the line:

```
140  STOP
```

and when the computer obeys this, it just stops and waits for your next command. If you want it to obey 500 to 560, you can enter

```
RUN 500
```

and it will start at line 500, and carry on until it finds a STOP instruction or runs out of stored instructions with line-numbers higher than 500.

Incidentally, if you have accumulated a whole load of rubbishy instructions in store, because you have been trying our various things, and you now want to get rid of them, just enter

```
NEW
```

and the effect will be the same as if you switched off, and switched on again.

You may want to do something less drastic, and clear the screen, without losing the instructions you have stored in the computer. To do this you enter the keyword

```
CLS
```

and the screen gets wiped clean. Any time you want to display the instructions in store you can do so by entering the keyword

```
LIST
```

or alternatively by pressing ENTER by itself.

Variables

When a data-value is stored and given a name, it is called a VARIABLE. This is because, once the name exists, you can change its value at any time, for example by using a new LET instruction. Try entering

```
LET A = 99
PRINT A
LET A = 23
PRINT A
```

The second LET instruction changed the value of the variable called A, so the second PRINT instruction caused the new changed value to be displayed. The same thing happens if you store the above four instructions (by re-entering them with line numbers) and then entering RUN.

Two-way conversations with the computer

One of the ingredients of a lively program is that it talks back to you and asks you questions while it is running. You can get your programs to do this, using the PRINT and the INPUT instructions. The INPUT instruction works like this. If you enter INPUT followed by the name of a variable, for example

```
INPUT x$
```

the computer waits for you to input the value of this variable. In this example, it is a character-type variable, because it ends with '$', so any character-string you type in will be accepted, for example

```
this*is?a!character!string#$-+
```

(followed by ENTER). If you next enter

```
PRINT x$
```

the same character-string will be displayed at the top of the screen.

By storing suitable PRINT and INPUT instructions, you can get the computer to conduct conversations which seem quite genuine. Try

```
100 PRINT "Hi ! my name is Pute" ' "Thats short for comPUTEr." ' "Would you mind telling me your name ?" ' "Just type it in and then press ENTER."
110 INPUT n$
120 PRINT n$ ' "Thats a marvellous name." ' "I like it" ' "When is your birthday?"
130 INPUT d$
140 PRINT "Your birthday is          "; d$ ;"      ?" ' "What a coincidence! Thats the same birthday as another friend of mine."
```

Notice the use of semicolons and apostrophes inthe PRINT instructions to control the display layout. You can try changing them. Notice also the use of the variable names n$ and d$ with INPUT and PRINT.

A useful item, which can actually be included in the list of items following PRINT, is TAB, followed by a number. TAB 11 means start printing the next item in column 11. (The columns in between are printed as spaces). If the line being printed was already beyond column 11, printing would continue on a new line.

```
PRINT 123 ; TAB 10 ; 456 ; TAB 20 ; 789
```

would print, all on one line

```
123      456       789
```

with the first digit of '123' in column 1, the first digit of '456' in column 10, and the first digit of '789' in column 20.

INPUT can be followed by a list of items, just as PRINT can, and the items must be separated using the same separators as with PRINT. But whatever separators are used, each item to be input must be followed by depressing the ENTER key, not by one of the separators.

If you want your program to display a message in the lower part of the screen, where the command lines are entered, you can do this by including the message in quotes in the INPUT list; for example:

```
100 INPUT "Enter your name and your age on separate lines" 'x$' y
110 PRINT x$,y
RUN
```

The computer will display the message at the bottom of the screen, and expect you to type your name followed by ENTER, then your age, followed by ENTER, and then it will display what you typed in on one line at the top of the screen, with age starting in column 17.

Here is a silly but fun program to convince anyone who is gullible enough to believe that the computer is a mind-reader.

```
500 PRINT "I can read your mind." ' "Think of a number." ' "Before you ENTER
it " ' "pull out the aerial lead" ' "between me and the television," ' "so that I can't
see" ' "what you type in ! " ''' "Then reconnect the aerial lead."
510 INPUT x$
520 CLS
530 PRINT "Now I shall tell you. " '' "The number you thought of, was" ',
540 PAUSE 500
550 PRINT x$
```

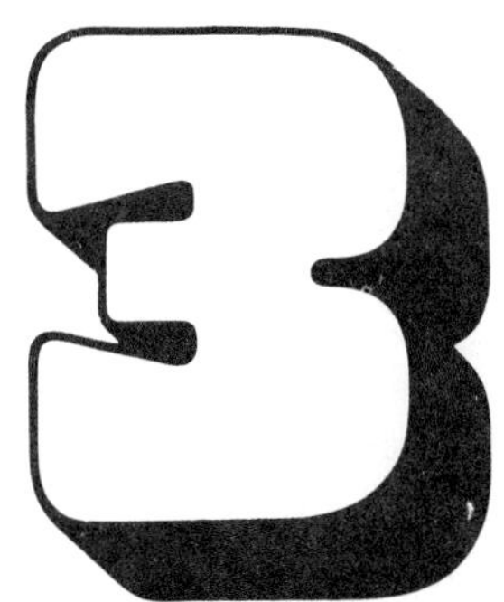

Going loopy

So far, every program we have looked at has been a straightforward sequence of instructions. Each instruction obeyed once and then on to the next until the last is reached and obeyed – and that's that. The idea of sequence underlies the very essence of the way the computer works. It is one of the most important of such underlying ideas. But it is not the only one.

Because the computer can *store* instructions, we can give it a special kind of instruction telling it which instruction to obey next. If we don't give it an instruction of that kind, then it just follows the SEQUENCE of stored instructions, using the line-numbers to determine the sequential order.

One of the easiest things to do is to get the computer to do something repeatedly, over and over again, a set number of times. For example, to get the computer to display the message 'HELLO THERE' say six times, we could use the following program

```
100  FOR k = 1 to 6
110  PRINT "HELLO THERE"
120  NEXT k
```

The variable *k* is called a control variable, because it is used to count and control the number of times the computer loops round these three instructions. The instructions which control the looping are 100 and 120. In line 100, *k* is assigned the starting value of 1, the first time round. Line 120 sends the computer back to line 100 and uses the NEXT value of *k*, that is, 2. This looping continues until the last time through, when *k* has achieved the value of 6. Then, when line 120 is reached, there is no next *k* so the loop is finished.

You can improve this program, that is make it more flexible, by changing it to

```
90   INPUT "Enter how many times" ' "you want me to say HELLO" ' N
100  FOR k = 1 to N
110  PRINT "HELLO THERE"
120  NEXT k
```

In the new version, the number of times, which is the value of *N*, is input while the program is running, so it can be different every time of running, without changing the program itself.

That was a very crude kind of loop, because exactly the same thing was done, on each repetition. We can use the same loop instructions to write a more useful loop – one that does something slightly different each time through, but different according to a well-formulated rule. For example, we can make use of the fact that each time through the loop, the control variable *k* has a value which is greater by 1 than the time before.

Suppose we want to add up all the integers from 1 to 100. Actually there is a simple formula we could use, which is easier than using a computer, but we'll do it just as an illustration of the technique. If you know the formula, you can use it to check the answer. If you don't then all the better!

The technique we use is the same as that used at a check-out cash register in the supermarket. First we assign the value zero to a variable we'll call *sum*, and then we write the loop. Inside the loop, we add the value of *k* to *sum* by saying

```
LET sum = sum + k
```

The complete program is

```
190  LET last = 100
200  LET sum = 0
210  For k = 1 to last
220  LET sum = sum + k
230  NEXT k
240  PRINT "the sum of all integers" ' "from 1 to "; last ; " is " ; sum
250  STOP
```

This program can be improved in a similar way to the last one, by changing line 190 to

```
190  INPUT "Enter value of last integer", last
```

If you want to see the way this program works, add another instruction to it

```
225  PRINT "value of k and current value of sum" ' k,sum
```

Making pretty patterns out of loops by putting loops in your program

It is easy to make pretty patterns on the screen, using the loop technique, and using the CIRCLE statement. The CIRCLE statement draws an entire circle for you.

Each time you use CIRCLE, you must specify where the centre is to be, and what the radius is. The position of the centre is specified by saying how far UP, and how far to the RIGHT it is of the bottom left-hand corner of the screen. For example

```
CIRCLE right, up, radius
```

will draw a circle on the screen provided we have already assigned values to *right, up* and *radius*. We have to be careful in doing this to make sure the circle doesn't go off the screen, else the program will fail. The bottom of the screen is 0 and the top is 175. The left of the screen is 0 and the far right is 255 (These are fixed values for this computer).

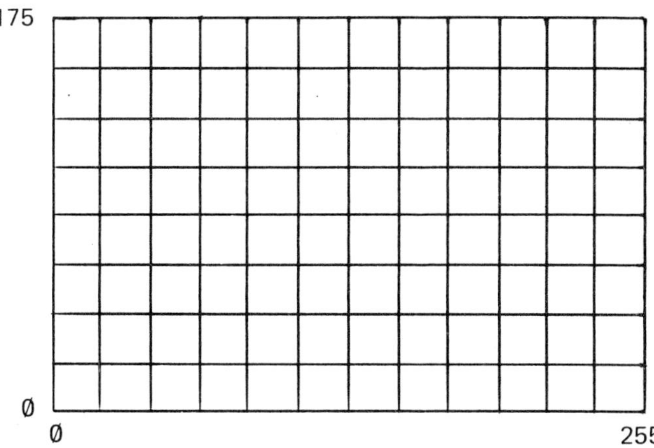

Your programming will be clearer and easier if you assign these values to variables right away, every time you want to make patterns on the screen. Then you can forget the actual numbers and let the computer deal with the arithmetic. It's better at it than you or I. For example:

```
10   LET upmax = 175
20   LET rightmax = 255
30   LET midup = 87
40   LET midright = 127
50   LET maxradius = midup
```

The largest circle we can draw on the screen is now obtained by the instruction

```
CIRCLE midright, midup, maxradius
```

But by using a loop, we can draw lots of circles with the same centre, but each with a different radius. How many circles? Lets leave it flexible.

```
100  INPUT "How many circles ? ", n
110  FOR k = 1 TO n
120  LET k ratio = k/n
130  LET radius = k ratio * maxradius
140  LET cenright = midright
150  LET cenup = midup
160  CIRCLE cenright, cenup, radius
170  NEXT k
```

Notice the technique of spreading the values of *radius* across the possible range by using the variable *k ratio*, the ratio of *k* to its maximum possible value *n*. This ratio increases as *k* increases, until it reaches the maximum value of 1. So we calculate *radius* by mutiplying *maxradius* by *k ratio*. That gives a nice even spread of the values the radius gets. The arithmetic is all left to the computer.

This technique is something you will need to use over and over again, so it is important to understand how it works. The best way is to run the following little demonstration program.

```
200  INPUT "value of n ?" , n
210  PRINT "when n= ", n
220  PRINT "k";TAB5; "k ratio" ' '
230  For k = 1 TO n
240  LET k ratio = k/n
250  PRINT k; TAB5 ; k ratio
260  NEXT k
```

If you run this a few times, choosing some simple values for *n*, like 3, 4, and 5 (and any others you fancy), you will see that the values calculated by the program for *k ratio* are exactly evenly spread out between 0 and 1, the first value always being $1/n$ and the last value, 1. The output produced when $n = 5$ is as follows:

when n = 5

k k ratio
1 0.2
2 0.4
3 0.6
4 0.8
5 1

No matter what value you choose for *n*, the values of *k ratio* are always automatically spaced out at equal intervals between 0 and 1.

But this is only half the story. Usually, we want some number, *n*, of equally spaced values spanning from 0 to some *MAX* value. A slight modification of the demonstration program will show how this is achieved.

Just add the lines

```
90   LET MAX = 40
245  LET spaced value = MAX * k ratio
```

and alter lines 220 and 250 to:

```
220  PRINT "k"; TAB5; "k ratio"; TAB20; "spaced value" ' '
250  PRINT k; TAB5; k ratio; TAB20; spaced value
```

If you run this modified program, and again use the value 5 for *n*, the output will be:

when n = 5

k	k ratio	spaced value
1	0.2	8
2	0.4	16
3	0.6	24
4	0.8	32
5	1	40

Try changing the value of *MAX*, and run this program several times, with different choices for *n*, and the way it works will show quite clearly.

Another point worth noticing is that additional variables *cenright* and *cenup* have been used in the line 160, with assignments to them in lines 140 and 150. There is good reason for this, as we shall see soon.

First try running this program, that is, enter lines 10 to 170 and run. Try varying the number of circles from say 10 to say 60.

Now to make the pattern more interesting, let's try moving the centre to the right when we draw each circle. Because of introducing the extra variable *cenright* in line 160, and assigning its value in line 140, we only have to change one line, 140 to do this, We can vary the position using the previously mentioned technique, tht is, multiplying *k ratio* by the maximum value we can go to the right of the screen. Now the nearest we can put the circle centre to the right-hand side is *maxradius*. That is to say, the maximum value that *cenright* can be is (*rightmax* – *maxradius*), so that is what we multiply by *k ratio* to get values for *cenright*. Therefore we change line 140 to

```
140  LET cenright = k ratio*(rightmax–maxradius)
```

If you still find it difficult to follow the arithmetic behind the expression used in line 140, add PRINT instructions so that the computer prints out its calculations each time while running the program. For example:

```
105  PRINT rightmax;" ";maxradius;" ";rightmax–maxradius
145  PRINT k ratio;" "; k ratio*maxradius
```

Line 105 gets obeyed just once, because it is placed before the loop begins; but line 145 is inside the loop, so it is obeyed once for each time the circle is to be drawn.

(SAVE this program. You will use some of it on page 34).

Building programs with prefabricated units

Subroutines

We are getting to the stage of developing useful pieces of program which we might want to incorporate in more than one program. There is a neat way of doing this, using what are called SUBROUTINES. As an illustration, take the instructions on lines 10 to 50, which set up inital values for the variables *upmax, rightmax,* and so on. They are likely to be useful for any program that draws circles or does any kind of drawing or plotting on the screen.

A subroutine is just another word for a sub-program. It can be called in and run at any point anywhere in the main program by using the instruction

GO SUB n

where n is the line-number of the first instruction in the subroutine, which has its own separate and different sequence of line numbers. At the end of the subroutine itself, we have to add an instruction that says merely

RETURN

The computer is clever enough to know where to return to because, whenever it obeys a GO SUB instruction, it stores the line-number of the following instruction, and that is where it goes back to when it hits RETURN.

Use of subroutines can make programs easier to read and understand, provided we insert remarks in our programs, both where a GO SUB is used and also at the beginning and end of the subroutine. A remark can be inserted on any line by starting with the keyword REM.

It is also useful to keep the line numbers used in subroutines well out of the way of the line-numbers you may want to use for main programs. So I would rewrite the program we have so far like this

```
50   REM **********************************
60   REM circle patterns program
70   REM ************************
80   LET starting values = 5000
90   GO SUB starting values
100  INPUT "How may circles ?", n
110  FOR k = 1 TO n
120  LET k ratio = k/n
130  LET radius = k ratio * maxradius
140  LET cenright = k ratio * ( rightmax – maxradius)
150  LET cenup = midup
160  CIRCLE cenright, cenup, radius
170  NEXT k
180  STOP
190  REM **********************************
5000 REM **********************************
5010 REM STARTING VALUES FOR DRAWING SUB
5020 REM **********************************
5030 LET upmax = 175
5040 LET rightmax = 255
```

```
5050 LET midup = 87
5060 LET midright = 127
5070 LET maxradius = midup
5100 RETURN
5110 REM **********************
```

The REM statements at lines 50, 70, 190, 5000, 5020, and 5110 are there to mark divisions which demarcate the separate pices of program, and to make the actual remarks stand out and catch the eye. This greatly improves the readability of programs, make them easier to follow, and easier to modify when the occasion arises. (It always does!)

Using colour

So far, we have not taken advantage of the opportunity to splash some colour around. This will not only make our pattern pretty but gives us another chance to see how useful subroutines can be.

One way of getting a variety of colour is to use the built-in function for generating random numbers. The function RND gives you a different random value between 0 and 1, every time you use it. Now the colours are coded as integers from 0 to 7, so the instruction

```
INK i
```

will change the colour of the ink used on the screen to the colour whose number is the current value of i. The colour codes are marked clearly above the top row of keys on the keyboard. We can get the computer to generate random integers by multiplying RND by a fairly large number. For no particular reason, I have chosen to use 257. As usual, I don't like using numbers. I prefer to use a meaningful name, so

```
LET anybigun = 257
LET i = INT(anybigun * RND)
```

Each time i is assigned a value, it will be an integer (whole-number) between 0 and 257. (The function INT takes the whole-number part of the value in brackets and throws away any fractional part.)

But the valid codes for colours are 0 to 7, and if we are going to draw on a white background (that is white PAPER), we could do well to stick to colours 1 to 5, because 6 is yellow and 7 is white. Ink of these colours doesn't show up very well on white paper (especially white ink).

When you want to change large numbers methodically so that they fit into a smaller range, one good way of doing it is to use the idea of REMAINDER after DIVISION.

Do this next little calculation with pencil and paper to get the idea.

Divide N by D;
take the INT of the result;
multiply by D;
then subtract the answer from N.

This gives you the remainder, and it always (must) have a value between 0 and $(D-1)$ inclusive. The remainder can't be D or bigger because you divided by D.

Once you get the hang of what to do, it is easy to express this calculation in the form of a single instruction.

```
LET Remainder = N – D*INT(N/D)
```

If you haven't followed this so far, get a pencil and paper. You be the computer and carry out the instruction yourself, using the pencil and paper and a couple of actual numbers, say 29 for *N*, and 7 for *D*. The calculation goes like this

(N/D) = 29/7 = $4\frac{1}{7}$
INT(N/D) = INT($4\frac{1}{7}$) = 4
D*INT(N/D) = 7*4 = 28
N–D*INT(N/D) = 29 – 28 = 1

Now try some other values for yourself, until you are happy with this formula.

This is a useful, even if small, piece of sub-progam, which may be handy to call upon at times in the future. But every time we want to use it, we may want to use it with a different pair of values for *N* and *D*. There is another program building block that is just right for this. It is called a FUNCTION. Before we can use a function, we have to write an instruction to define it. This instruction always starts with the keyword DEF FN (CAPS SHIFT and SYMBOL SHIFT followed by SYMBOL SHIFT and 1) DEF FN stands for 'definition of a function'. You can choose any name you like for the function but it has to be a single letter (upper- or lower-case). The name comes straight after the keyword and is followed by a pair of brackets which enclose a list of names for the values (separated by commas) that we want the function to use. So the instruction to define a function called *R* for Remainder would be

```
DEF FN R(N,D) = N – D*INT(N/D)
```

Once that has been obeyed in the program, it can be used. For example, to assign a value in ink colour, using the random number method we could have

```
LET anybigun = 257
LET bigrandom = INT (Anybigun * RND)
LET i = FN R(bigrandom, 6)
```

Notice that when the function is used, as opposed to defined, the keyword needed is FN, instead of DEF FN. I have used 6 for *D* to make sure of producing a colour ink that shows on white paper, that is, a colour value ranging from 0 to 5 inclusive.

We can put all this together into a subroutine so that every time we need a random colour, all we have to write is GO SUB 5990

```
5990 REM **********************
6000 REM random colour SUB
6010 REM **********************
6020 DEF FN R(N,D) = N – D*INT(N/D)
6030 LET anybigun = 257
6040 LET bigrandom = INT (anybigun*RND)
```

```
6050 INK FN R(bigrandom, 6)
6060 RETURN
6070 REM **********************
```

We can bring this subroutine into our circle patterns program by adding to that program the line

```
155   GO SUB 5990
```

Using one line-number for more than one instruction

It is worth mentioning that instead of just one instruction per line-number, the computer will accept two or more instructions so long as we separate the instructions with the colon-symbol. For example, we could follow the GO SUB instruction on line 155 by a remark

```
155 GO SUB 5990: REM random colour
```

Inserting REM statements in this way helps program readability. However, if you do use the colon-symbol to write several commands with one line-number make sure that only the last one is a REM statement. Otherwise, the computer will assume the colon *after* it is not after it but part of it. Everything following REM will be treated as comment until the next line-number is encountered. An alternative and useful way of achieving the same object – to make the program easier to read, follow and understand – is to rewrite line 155 this way:

```
155   LET random colour = 5990: GO SUB random colour
```

Looping through data values and making selections

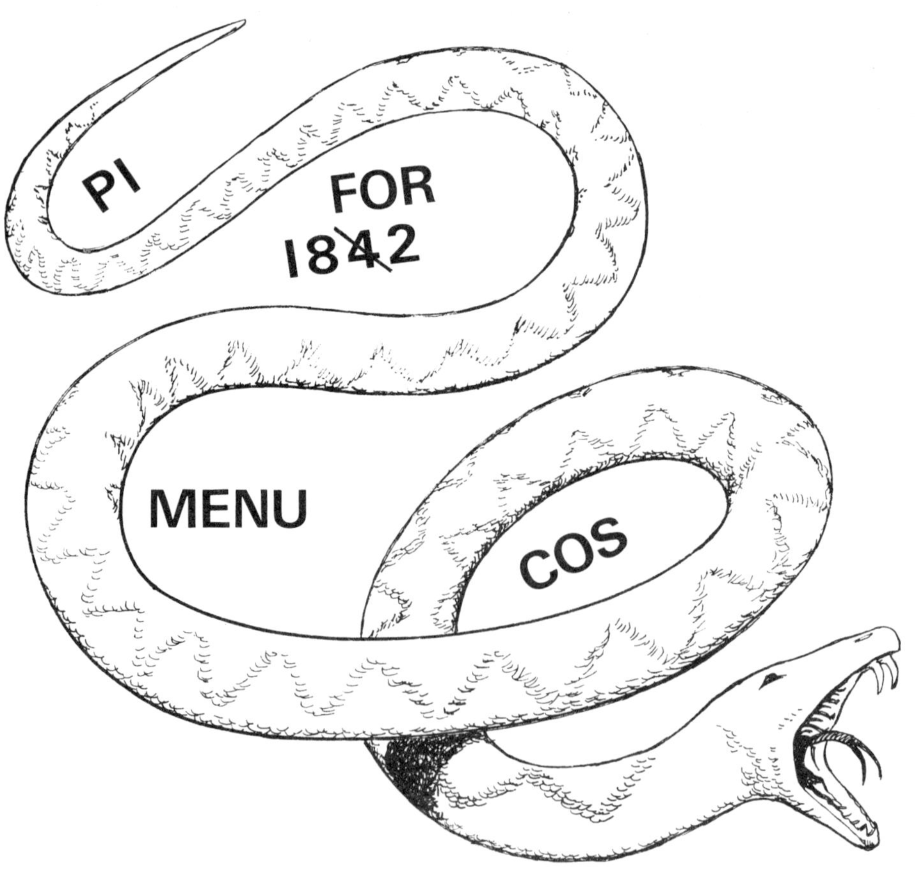

Arrays

We have seen pretty loops (circles) displayed on the screen in many colours, and control loops built into programs. A loop in a program goes through a sequence of instructions, but sometimes we want to use such a program loop to go through a sequence of data values.

There is a way of naming a sequence of data-values which makes it easier to process them (one at a time) each time round a program loop. If each data item has a completely different name this can't be done, so there is a way of giving them all a common name, and then distinguishing each item by an integer in brackets after the name. This is called an array. The number in brackets, that distinguishes each array element, is called the index or subscript.

For example, if we had say 15 numerical data-items, and wanted to put them in an array, we can choose any single letter as the name of the array. If we choose X, then the first item will be called $X(1)$, the second $X(2)$, the third $X(3)$, the eleventh $X(11)$, and the last one $X(15)$. Each individual name can be used just like any other variable. But the real utility of this system of naming comes from the fact that we can write any expression we like inside the brackets, so long as the computer will accept it as an expression which can be evaluated as an integer.

If we are writing a loop whose control variable is, say, j, then inside the loop, if we wish, we can write instructions that refer to $X(j)$ or $X(j+1)$ or $X(2*j)$ and so on. Each time through the loop, j gets a different value.

Even when we do want a loop to process a sequence of data-items, we don't need an array if we are only going to use the data-items one at a time, finishing with each one before going on to the next. For example, to add up a long sequence of numbers we don't need an array.

```
100 LET sum = 0
110 FOR d = 1 to 10
120 INPUT "enter next number", nextval
130 LET sum = sum + nextval
140 NEXT d
150 PRINT "sum = "; sum
160 STOP
```

But if we wanted to sort a set of values into ascending numerical order, we should want them all in store at the same time, and an array would be required.

Before using an array, you have to tell the computer its name and how big it is. This is so that the computer can organize the space in store to keep all the values. The instruction for telling the computer is called a DIM statement. This is not so silly as it sounds. DIM stands for DIMension of the array. If you want an array with 99 individual data-values in it, called say B, you say

```
100 DIM B(99)
```

Then you can use $B(1), B(2), \ldots B(99)$ as variables. If we want to build a program to sort numbers into ascending order, we shall probably have a different number of values to sort on different occasions. However, it's not necessary to change the DIM statement, because the computer allows us to write

```
100 INPUT "how many values ?", N
110 DIM B(N)
```

This means that when the program is run, first you enter the number of values, and then the values themselves

```
120  FOR k = 1 to N
130  INPUT "enter next value", B(k)
140  NEXT k
```

When that loop has been run, all N values will have been entered and stored, the first in $B(1)$, the second in $B(2)$ and so on, because the first time through the loop, k has the value 1 so $B(k)$ is $B(1)$; the second time through, k has the value 2, so $B(k)$ is $B(2)$. That's how it works.

There are countless ways of sorting values. Some methods are very fast. Other are very slow. The easiest one to understand and program is just about the slowest. We'll use it here because its the easiest. It uses two program loops, one inside the other. The inside loop goes through all the values in the array looking for the smallest. Then the smallest value is swapped for the one at the beginning. There are two phases here. The first is finding the smallest item (needing a loop). The second is swapping the smallest and first. Both these phases are put in the outside loop, which runs these two phases again, but missing out the first item, because we know it is the smallest. On this second time, the smallest item in the rest of the array is swapped with the second item in the array. So each time through the outer loop, there are fewer items left to sort. Eventually there are none – the whole array is sorted.

IF . . . THEN . . . instructions

Now, before we can build the sorting program, there is another programming mechanism we shall want to use. It is a program mechanism for selecting between two different possible program actions, where the decision is based on a comparison you instruct the computer to make. This instruction starts with the keyword IF, is followed by a condition whose truth you want the computer to test, and next comes the keyword THEN, followed in the same line by a new instruction which is obeyed if and only if the condition was found to be true. So the instruction has the form

IF test-condition THEN conditional instruction

Here is a little program which tests whether a number that is input is negative or not.

```
10   INPUT "enter any number, positive, negative or zero", x
20   IF x < 0 THEN GO TO 50
30   PRINT x, "is not negative"
40   GO TO 60
50   PRINT x, "is negative"
60   STOP
```

There is yet another instruction in that example, the GO TO instruction. Its meaning is very straightforward. When obeyed, it interrupts the normal sequencing of instructions and sends the computer off to the specified line-number.

I call this piece of program a decision box. The structure of this piece of program is most important. Unless you understand it you will find the use of IF most confusing. I want to emphasize the structure by a program pattern diagram.

Program pattern boxes

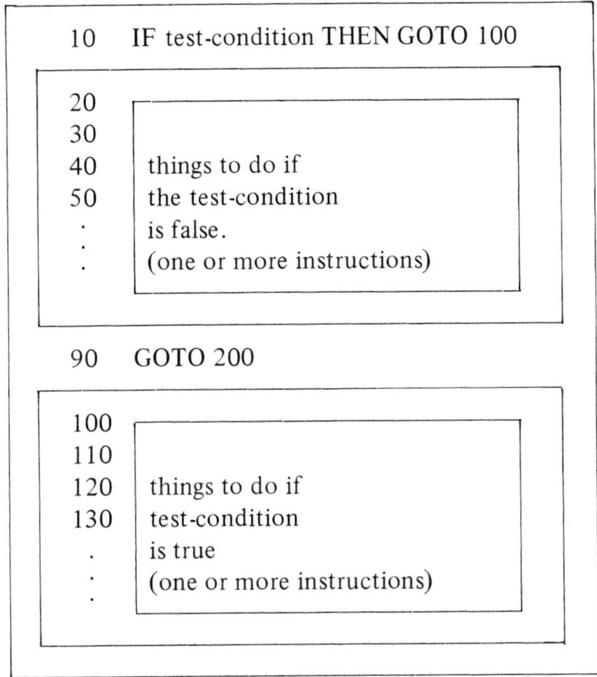

200 next-program-instruction-after the decision-box

Program-pattern of decision-box 1

This should be used as a pattern every time you want to program a choice between two sets of actions.

There are cases where the choice is not between two actions, but between taking some action, or alternatively doing nothing. Then the diagram reduces to a simplified form because the second inner box can disappear and so can the unconditional GOTO (the one on line 90 in the diagram). The simplified pattern becomes

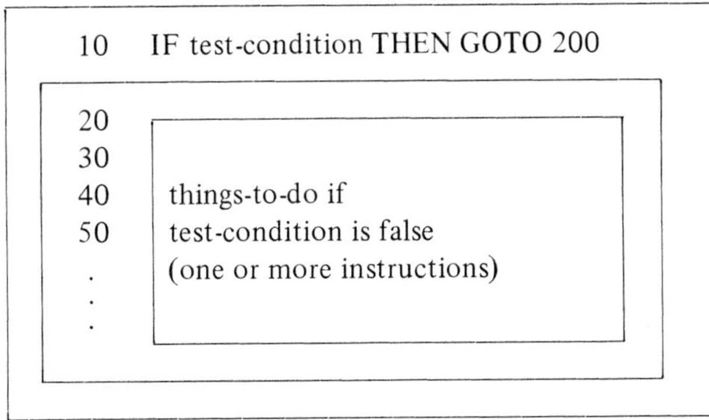

200 next-program-instruction after the decision-box

Program-pattern of decision-box 2

These two program-patterns for decision boxes will be used over and over again in almost every program.

Notice that box 2 contains just *one* IF and *one* GO TO, while box 1 contains just *one* IF and *two* GO TOs. When you are constructing a decision box in one of your own programs, check firstly which kind of box it is. Then count how many IFs and how many GO TOs you have used. If you have used more than necessary, *throw it away and start again.* Don't try to alter it! It is much easier to get it right from scratch than to change a muddle to make it right.

Now we are ready to tackle the sorting program. We shall start by looking at the inner loop. First we assign the value 1 to a variable called *smallest*, because, before we look at any other values, $B(1)$ is the smallest so far. Then comes a loop from 2 to N, in which we shall test whether $B(k)$ is smaller than $B(smallest)$.

```
200  LET smallest = 1
210  FOR k = 2 TO N

220  IF B(smallest)< B(k) THEN GOTO 240

230  LET smallest = k

240  NEXT k
250  REM smallest value is in B(smallest)
```

Lines 220 and 230 have the pattern of decision box 2. Every time through the loop, this piece of program changes the value of *smallest* to the current value of k whenever it finds that $B(k)$ is smaller than the smallest item so far, which is $B(smallest)$. If $B(smallest) < B(k)$ is *not true* it does nothing, and loops round to the next value of k.

So it goes through the entire array just once, starting at 2, and comes out with *smallest* having the value of the index of the smallest item in the array.

Next we need to swap $B(smallest)$ with $B(1)$. It is worth pointing out that the next two lines don't work!

```
10   LET B(1) = B(smallest)
20   LET B(smallest) = B(1)
```

Why not? Because by the time the program gets to the second line, the original value of $B(1)$ has been lost! To do a swap we need to keep hold of that value. The next three lines do it

```
10   LET keephold = B(1)
15   LET B(1) = B(smallest)
20   LET B(smallest) = keephold
```

If you don't follow this, place three sheets of paper in front of you. Mark one $B(1)$, the second $B(smallest)$ and the third *keephold*. Place two coins of different value, the smallest on $B(1)$ and the larger on $B(smallest)$. Since $B(smallest)$ has the wrong coin, we have to swap them.

Translating the three computer instructions to fit the parable

10 Move coin from $B(1)$ to *keephold*
15 Move coin from $B(smallest)$ to $B(1)$
20 Move coin from *keephold* to $B(smallest)$

Now to recap, we have a piece of program which goes through the array, picks out the smallest element, and swaps it with the first element.

We want to keep repeating that piece of program, with a small but important difference each time. The first time the loop began with

```
FOR k = 1 TO N
```

and after finishing, swapped $B(smallest)$ with $B(1)$.

But the second time, we want it to begin with

```
FOR k = 2 TO N
```

and after finishing, swap $B(smallest)$ with $B(2)$.

The third time, we want

```
FOR k = 3 TO N
```

and after finishing the loop, swap $B(smallest)$ with $B(3)$.

In fact if the *starting value* for k was a variable, say j, we could say that EVERY time we perform this piece of program, we want the loop to begin

```
FOR k = j TO N
```

and after finishing the loop, we want to swap $B(smallest)$ with $B(j)$.

How many and for what values of j do we want to run through this piece of program? Well, the first time we want $j = 1$, and the last time we want $j = N$. So all we need to do is to put the whole piece of program inside another loop controlled by j. Like this:

```
70  INPUT "how many values ?", N
80  DIM B(N)
90  FOR z = 1 To N : INPUT "next value", B(z) : NEXT z

100 FOR j = 1 TO N
110 REM ************************************

120 REM here comes the program that finds the smallest element
140 LET smallest = j
150 FOR k = j TO N
160 IF B(smallest) < B(k) THEN GOTO 180
170 LET smallest = k
180 NEXT k
190 REM smallest value in B(j) to B(N) now in B(smallest)

200 REM ************************************

210 REM here comes the swap between B(j) and B(smallest)
220 LET keephold = B(j)
230 LET B(j) = B(smallest)
240 LET B(smallest) = keephold
250 REM swap done

260 REM ************************************
270 REM the array B from 1 to j so far is now sorted
280 NEXT j

290 REM ************************************
300 REM whole array B is now sorted
310 REM ************************************
320 PRINT "index" , "sorted values" ' ': FOR z = 1 To N : PRINT z, B(z) : NEXT z
```

The boxes drawn around pieces of this program contain the pieces of program we developed separately and then used to build the program out of them.

This is the sensible way to make programs. As the programs you write get bigger, it becomes necessary to draw the boxes first, before you start writing any program. Otherwise your program will be a complete muddle, and it is unlikely to do what you want it to do. If you think about this for a moment it is not surprising. Imagine trying to build a house without making any planning decisions first, like how many rooms it should have and how big they are to be and what they will be used for, and so on.

Programs need the same kind of planning, and it is called program design. We even talk about the structure of programs, just as though they were houses.

Of course, everyone knows what a house is, knows what it is for, has lived in one, so it is possible to discuss house design without ever having mixed concrete or stuck bricks together with mortar.

Program design is similar once you are as familiar with programs, as you are with houses. But first of all, in the case of programs, you need to learn how to make the building blocks, and how to stick them together. That is why program pattern diagrams and drawing boxes round pieces of program are so important.

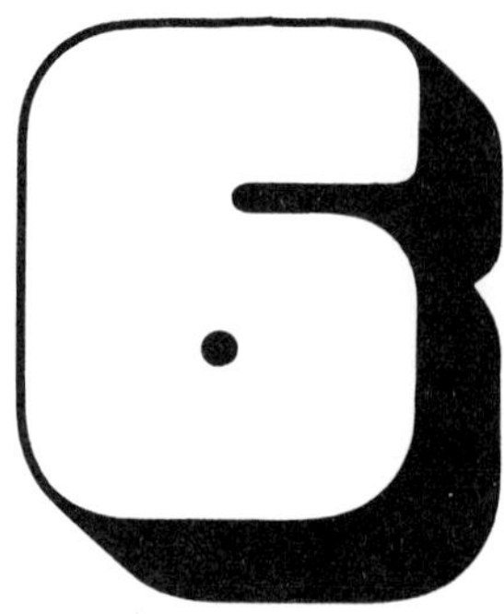

Roundabouts and rings

Going round in circles

If you don't mind using a bit of mathematical know-how, an interesting pattern-creating program can be built, using circles as a basis.

There is of course, the CIRCLE instruction that was exploited in Chapter 3 and 4. But supposing that didn't exist, how would you draw a circle? And even though it does exist, how would you draw a number of circles whose centres lie evenly spaced around the circumference of a circle?

– like this:

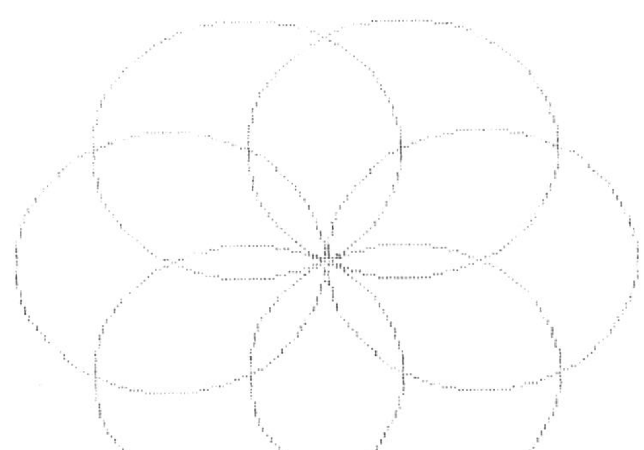

or like this:

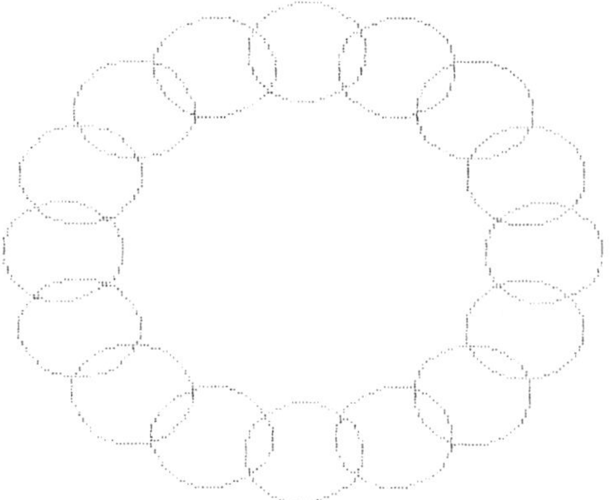

First let us take a look at the instructions we shall be using – PLOT, and DRAW. The instruction

PLOT right, up

plots a point on the screen, using the values of *right* and *up* the same way that CIRCLE uses them:

Ø <= *right* <= 255
Ø <= *up* <= 175

So one new way of drawing a circle would be to plot points, very close together, which lie in a circle. We can do this if we know the mathematical relation between the values of *up* and *right* and the radius and centre of the circle we want to draw. Suppose we want to draw a circle whose centre is at the centre of the screen, that is, at the point (*midright, midup*), and with radius given by the variable *r*.

The basic mathematics is not too difficult, and is easier to follow if you draw a little diagram. Take any point you like on the circumference of a circle and join it to the centre by a straight line, and then construct a right-angled triangle whose hypotenuse is that straight line, and with one of the other two sides lying along the horizontal diameter. Your diagram of circle and triangle should now look something like this:

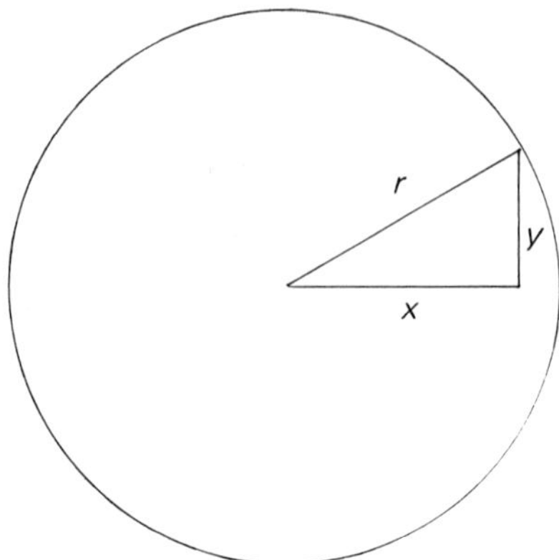

or this:

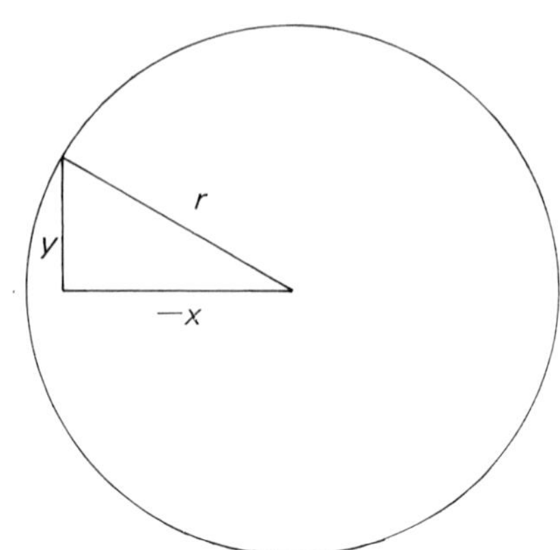

or like this:

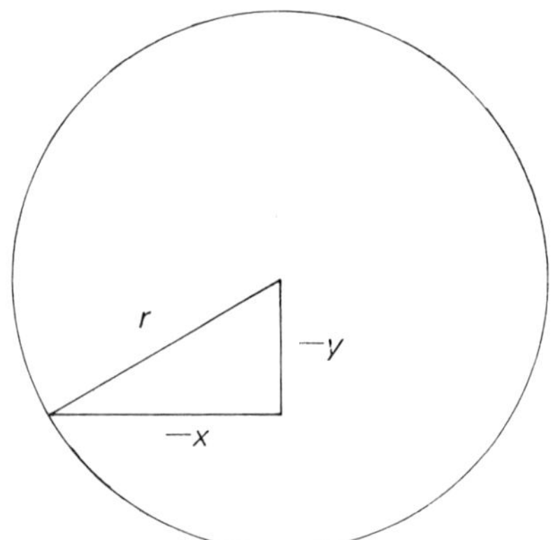

or this:

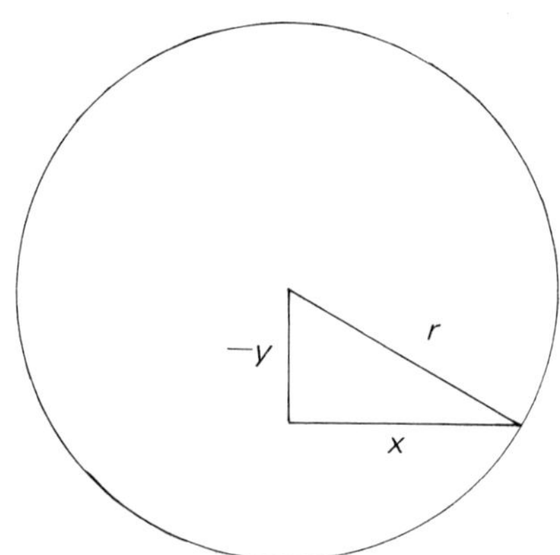

In every case, as was discovered long ago by a talented Greek named Pythagoras, if you take the square of the length of the hypotenuse (the longest side), that square is equal to the sum of the squares of the other two sides. In our four cases:

$$x^2 + y^2 = r^2$$
$$(-x)^2 + y^2 = r^2$$
$$(-x)^2 + (-y)^2 = r^2$$
$$x^2 + (-y)^2 = r^2$$

As you can see, it turns out that the sign of x or y doesn't matter, so we shall stick to the first case. If we divide each term in the equation by r^2 we can rewrite it as

$$(x/r)^2 + (y/r)^2 = 1$$

Now when x and y are the two short sides of a right-angled triangle whose long side is r, mathematicians call the ratio (x/r) the SINE of *theta*, and the ratio (y/r) the COSINE of *theta*, shortening each of these to SIN(*theta*) and COS(*theta*) where *theta* (a letter of the Greek alphabet) is the size of the angle between the sides of length *x* and *r*. (It is only fair to use a Greek letter, to show proper respect for Pythagoras).

The mathematical functions SIN and COS are built-in functions of the computer. So with a little juggling, we can re-arrange our circle equation into two parts:

(1) $x = r * \text{COS}\ (theta)$
(2) $y = r * \text{SIN}\ (theta)$

and those are the formulae we shall use to plot points in a circle. We can use values of *theta* evenly spaced between the extreme values Ø and 2*PI, because, in radian measure of angle, as used by the computer (*not* degrees), 2*PI is the angle equivalent to one complete rotation, the equivalent of 360 degrees.

Of course, if you plot points with the values for *x* and *y* straight from formula (1) and formula (2), the points will lie in a circle around the bottom left-hand corner of the screen. Some of them would be off the screen, and the program would crash. We have to add to *x*, and to *y*, the values of *right* and *up* which gives the place on the screen where we want the circle centre to be.

So even if you are not interested in *how* the expressions for *x* and *y* were derived, it is quite easy to *use* them. How many points would you like to plot in a circle?

```
500  INPUT "how many points ? "; n
510  INPUT "value of radius, up to 40 ? "; r
520  LET angle = 2*PI/n
530  FOR k = 1 TO n
540  LET theta = k*angle
550  LET x = midright + r*COS(theta)
560  LET y = midup + r*SIN(theta)
570  PLOT x, y
580  NEXT k
```

If you make *n* as great as 500, the points will be plotted so close together they will form a continuous circle. With *n* equal to say 100, they will form a circle of dots on the screen.

Now that gives us a basis for doing something more interesting. For a start, we could change line 570, which plots a point, to

```
570  CIRCLE x, y, small r
```

where *small r* is the radius of a (smaller) circle to be drawn with centre at (*x*, *y*). We shall need to add another INPUT statement at the beginning so that the value of *small r* can be input.

There are other changes we can make which will give a wider variety of pretty patterns. One of these is to change the large circle followed round the screen into an ellipse. This is easy. All that is required is to flatten either the *x* or the *y* value by a constant factor which lies between Ø and 1. This factor is really the *aspect* from which a circle can be viewed. The nearer its value is to 1, the nearer to a circle the ellipse will be. The smaller the *aspect* value, the flatter the ellipse will be. If the *aspect* vaule is zero, the ellipse flattens into a straight line, like looking at a circle edge on.

To keep the choices wide open, the value of *aspect* can be input too, and an extra line inserted

565 LET y = aspect*y

Yet another variation which is easy to introduce is to make a slight reduction in the radius of the small circles, each time before the next one is drawn. Again, an extra INPUT instruction is needed at the beginning, and another extra line to reduce *r* each time through the loop.

575 LET r = reduction*r

And a final simple variation is to have the program make more than one circuit, the number of circuits to make being another input value. The number of circuits is used to multiply the total angle. That is, if *2*PI* is 1 circuit, then *2*PI*c* is *c* circuits.

A complete program developed along these lines follows; and after the listing are some examples of the patterns you can get it to make, using the input values given.

```
100>REM ************ circles program ************
110 GO SUB 300: REM data input
120 GO SUB 400: REM init vals
130 GO SUB 500: REM do pattern
140 GO SUB 600: REM re-run ?
150 STOP : REM end of main program *************

300 REM data input SUBr *************************
310 INPUT "no of circuits ?  ";circuits
320 INPUT "no of circles ?  ";n
330 INPUT "aspect ratio<=1 ?  ";aspect
340 IF (aspect>1) OR (aspect<0) THEN  INPUT "inva
lid value"'"Hit ENTER & try again";a$: GO TO 330
350 INPUT "starting radius<=79 ?  ";initr
360 IF (initr>79) OR (initr<0) THEN  INPUT "inval
id value"'"Hit ENTER & try again";a$: GO TO 350
370 INPUT "radius reduction ratio ?  ";reduc
380 IF (reduc>1) OR (reduc<=0) THEN  INPUT "inval
id value"'"Hit ENTER & try again";a$: GO TO 370
390 RETURN : REM ******************************

400 REM initial values SUBr *********************
410 BRIGHT 1: INK 0: PAPER 6: CLS
420 LET angle=2*PI*circuits/n
430 LET ymid=88: LET xmid=127: LET r=initr
```

```
 440 LET Rx=xmid-initr
 450 LET Ry=ymid-initr-8: REM (-8) to leave room f
or printing on screen
 460 LET yxratio=Ry/Rx: REM andscale pattern to fi
ll screen
 470 IF aspect>yxratio THEN  LET Rx=Ry/aspect: REM
 reduce Rx to aspect ratio
 480 IF aspect<yxratio THEN  LET Ry=Rx*aspect: REM
 reduce Ry to aspect ratio
 490 RETURN : REM ********************************

 500 REM do pattern SUBr *************************
 505 LET tab=28: PRINT "input data:"'"circuits";TA
B tab+2;circuits'"circles";TAB tab+2;n;AT 18,0;"as
pect";TAB tab;aspect'"radius";TAB tab;initr'"reduc
";TAB tab;reduc
 510 FOR k=1 TO n
 520 LET theta=k*angle
 530 LET y=ymid+Ry*SIN (theta)
 540 LET x=xmid+Rx*COS (theta)
 550 CIRCLE x,y,r
 560 LET r=reduc*r
 570 NEXT k
 590 RETURN : REM ********************************
 600 REM re-run ? SUBR ***************************
 610 INPUT "Rerun? hit ENTER.Else STOP";c$
 620 IF c$="" THEN  GO TO 100
 630 RETURN : REM ******** end of program ********
```

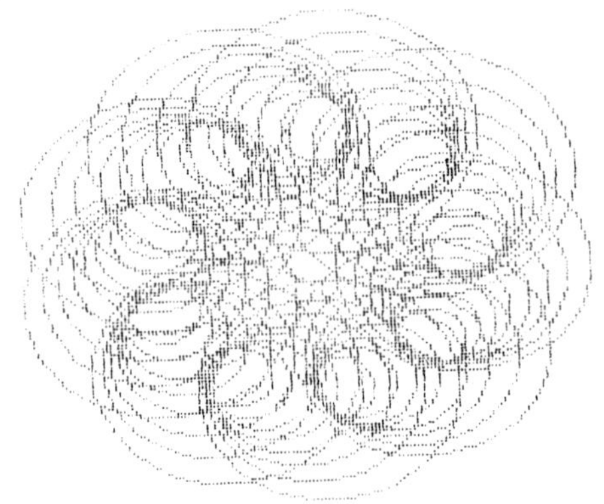

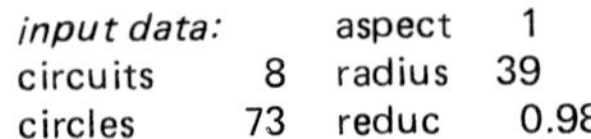

input data:		aspect	1
circuits	8	radius	39
circles	73	reduc	0.98

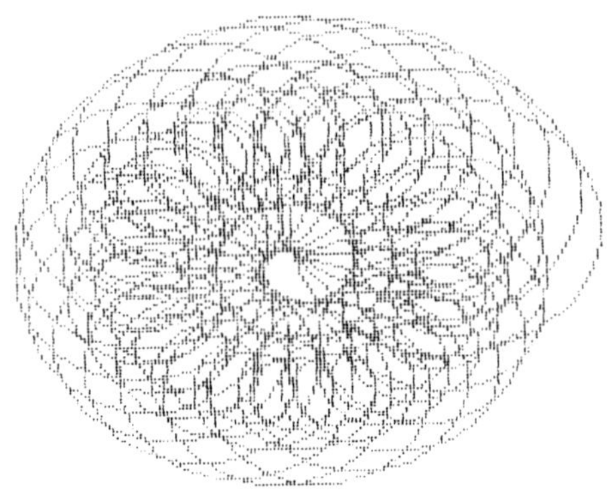

input data:		aspect	1
circuits	3	radius	40
circles	70	reduc	0.98

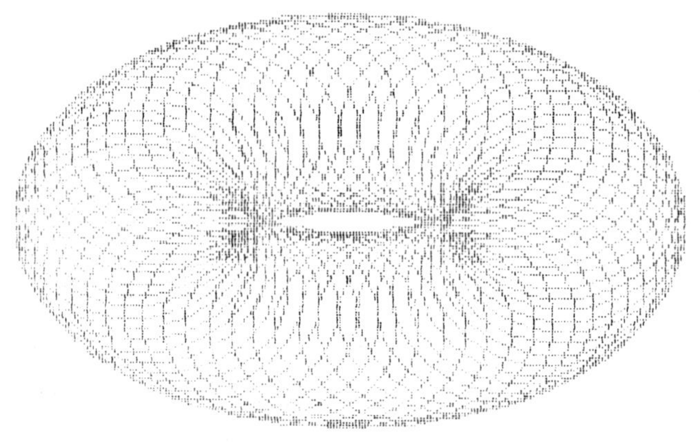

input data:		aspect	0.6
circuits	1	radius	38
circles	60	reduc	1

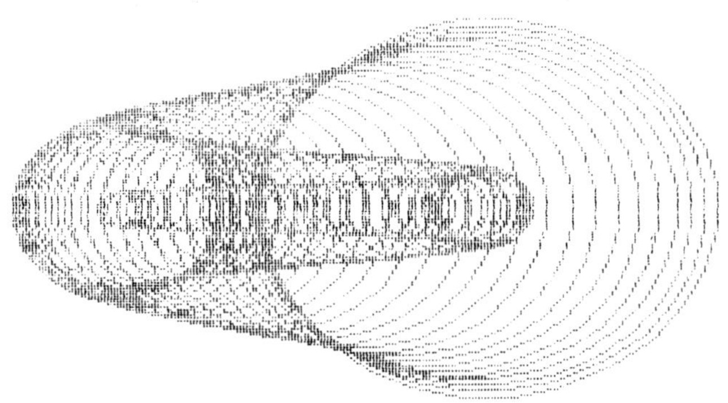

input data:		aspect	0
circuits	1.5	radius	70
circles	80	reduc	0.97

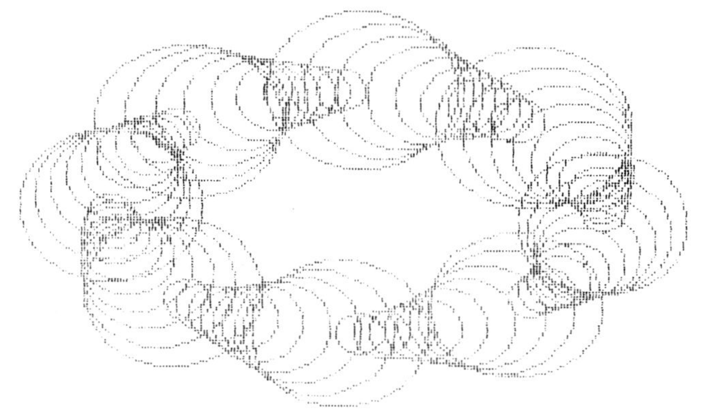

input data:		aspect	0.6
circuits	9	radius	32
circles	73	reduc	0.98

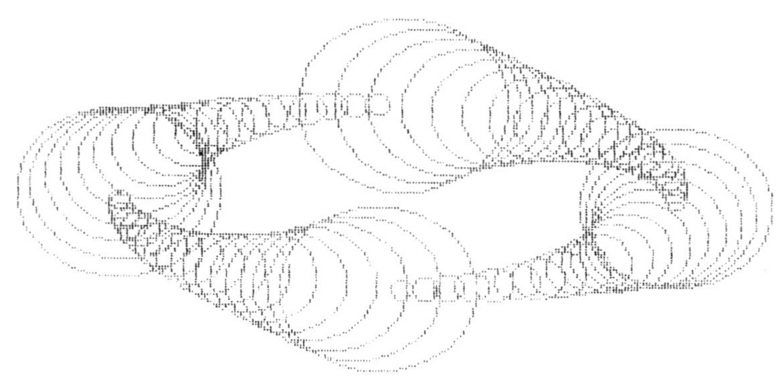

input data:		aspect	0.4
circuits	18	radius	35
circles	73	reduc	0.97

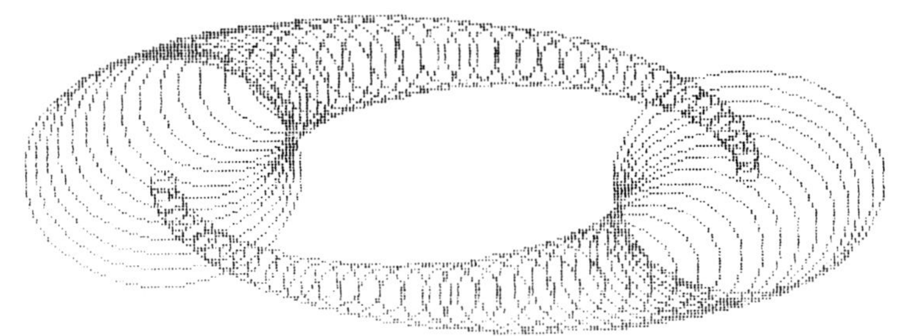

input data:		aspect	0.5
circuits	40	radius	39
circles	81	reduc	0.97

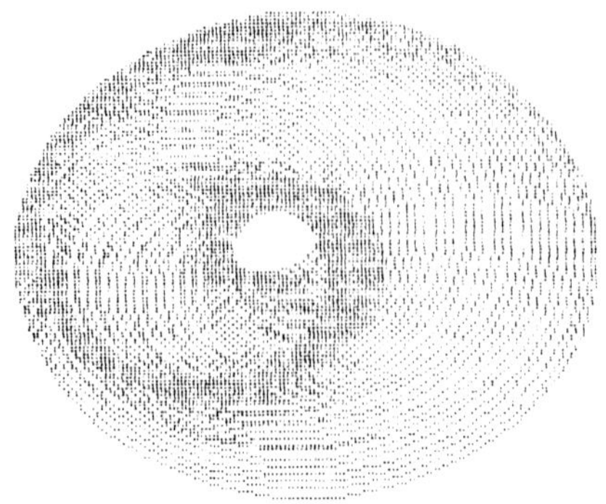

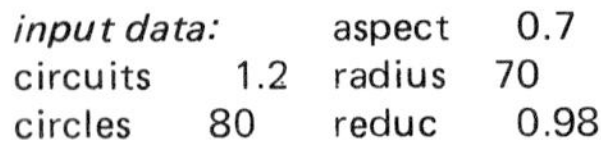

input data: aspect 0.7
circuits 1.2 radius 70
circles 80 reduc 0.98

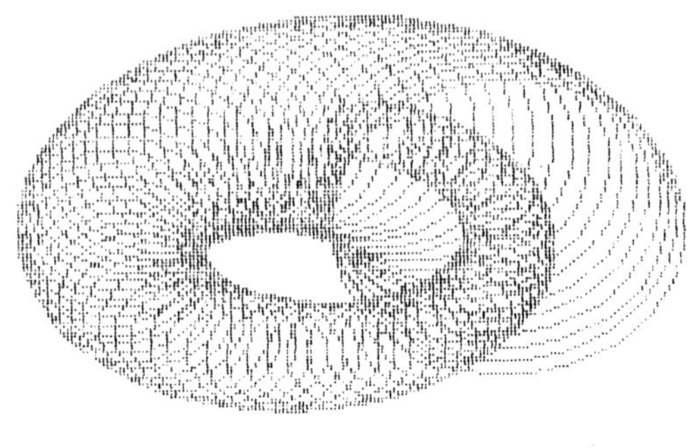

input data: aspect 0.7
circuits 1.2 radius 45
circles 80 reduc 0.98

You can't get anywhere without pulling strings

How long is a (piece of) string?

As well as arrays of numbers, you can have arrays of character-strings. Now one element of an array of number-values is just like an ordinary number-variable.

However, one element of a string array is not quite like an ordinary string variable, because the length of an array element is fixed to be the same as the length of all the other elements in the array. Furthermore, each element itself can be regarded as an array of characters. The result of this is that a string array has two integers in brackets after its name. The first integer tells you which *string* in the array. The second tells you which *character* in the *string*. If we are not particularly interested in individual characters, only in whole strings, we can leave out the second integer in the brackets. But we MUST include BOTH in the DIM statement. As you might expect, the name you are allowed to choose for a string array is a single letter followed by the dollar symbol. For example

```
100 DIM H$(8, 43)
```

but you may prefer to say

```
100 LET strlen = 43
110 LET arraylen = 8
120 DIM H$(arraylen, strlen)
```

I have chosen (8, 43) because the example I'm going to work with has eight strings, which I want in an array (so I can loop through them); and the longest STRingLENgth is 43 characters long. It's OK to use a shorter string. The computer pads it out with spaces at the end. This example shows how you can get the computer to process words, in a very simple way of course. Up to now we can only tackle kid stuff, so why not build a nursery rhyme.

First piece of program is a chore. It assigns the strings I want to use.

```
300 LET H$(1) = " the man all tattered and torn, who kissed"
310 LET H$(2) = " the maiden all forlorn, who milked"
320 LET H$(3) = " the cow with the crumpled horn, that tossed"
330 LET H$(4) = " The dog, that worried"
340 LET H$(5) = " The cat, that killed"
350 LET H$(6) = " The rat, that ate"
360 LET H$(7) = " the malt that lay in"
370 LET H$(8) = " the house that Jack built."
380 LET a$ = " This is"
```

I want to write a program that will display the whole nursery rhyme, which has a well-defined structure that makes the whole thing easy. . .

This is the structure
That lies behind
the nursery rhyme
that lay in the house
that Jack built!

(sorry, I got carried away).

The first verse is $a\$, H\$(8)$
The second verse is $a\$, H\$(7), H\$(8)$
The third verse is $a\$, H\$(6), H\$(7), H\$(8)$
The fourth verse is $a\$, H\$(5), H\$(6), H\$(7), H\$(8)$

and so on until

the eighth verse is $a\$, H\$(1), H\$(2), \ldots H\$(8)$

There is a fairly obvious pattern about this. Each verse consists of *a*$ followed by a number of the *H*$ strings. For the first verse it is one of them, for the fifth verse five of them, for the eight verse, eight of them. In fact, if we called the verse number *k*, then for each verse, the first string to be printed after *a*$ will always be:

one more than eight minus *k*

The reason for eight is that it is the total number of strings in the array *H*$, that is, *arraylen*. So a more computerised way of saying this is that for the *k*th verse, the first string to be printed after *a*$ is

H$(*arraylen* + 1 − *k*)

and the last to be printed is

H$(*arraylen*)

So to print out the *k*th verse, we need first to print *a*$, and then a loop to print out the elements of *H*$

```
500  REM to print out kth verse
510  PRINT a$
520  FOR j = arraylen + 1 - k TO arraylen
530  PRINT H$(j)
540  NEXT j
550  REM the kth verse has now been printed
```

We could even make this a subroutine, by adding

```
560  RETURN
```

If we do that, then all that's needed to complete the program is to add the lines

```
200  FOR k = 1 TO arraylen
210  GO SUB 500
220  NEXT k
230  STOP
```

and also insert the lines

```
130  GO SUB 300
390  RETURN
```

When you run this program, you will notice that the output displayed is not as neat as you might wish. There are two sources of trouble. The first is that some lines are longer than the width of the screen (32 characters). There isn't much to be done about that. The second is that there appear to be lots of blank lines where there shouldn't be. This is because, as far as the computer is concerned, EVERY string in the array *H$* is longer than the screen width because each one is 43 characters long. The fact that many of them end with a string of spaces hides this fact from the human eye. But the computer prints out the spaces just as merrily as all other characters, and they spill over on the next line, thus giving a blank line.

There is an easy way to overcome this second problem, but it involves something called slicing, so we'll have a look at that, because it is very useful and easy to use.

Slicing Character Strings

The DIM statement for the array *H$* was

```
DIM H$(arraylen, strlen)
```

The quantities in the brackets are called subscripts, or array indexes, because they index the array. Up until now we haven't used the second index, only the first. The first indexes the actual strings. The second indexes the characters in the string.

So *H$*(2, 6) is the character 'm', because that's the sixth character in the second string (the initial letter of 'maiden').

Some of the strings that were assigned to *H$* were comparatively short. For example, the string assigned to *H$*(6) has only 17 characters, yet *H$*(6) has room for 43 bytes. The computer takes care of this by assigning spaces to the bytes left over.

Now slicing is a way of taking a slice out of a whole string. If we want to PRINT only the original string assigned to *H$*(6), which was 17 characters long, and not be encumbered with the spaces that were filled in, we can say

```
PRINT H$(6, 1 TO 17)
```

This uses the expression 1 TO 17 in the place where the character index goes, and it means exactly what it says – characters 1 TO 17. If for some queer reason we wished to print only the spaces that were filled in at the end of the string, we could say

```
PRINT H$(6, 18 TO 43)
```

The only remaining problem is to write instructions to count the number of spaces the computer used to 'pad out' the string to its full length. This is not difficult. We need a loop in which we look at the string, character by character, starting at the end and working backwards, and testing to see if there is a space.

We keep a note of the reduced length of the string in a variable I call *UPLen* (to stand for UnPaddedLength).

We start by assuming that the unpadded length is equal to the full length, and reduce it by 1 for every character that is a space, until we reach one that isn't. The easy way to do this is to assign the value of the loop control variable to *UPLen* at the beginning of the loop, each time through. Immediately after that, we use an IF statement to test whether the *z*th character is a space. If it is we carry on with the loop. As soon as the *z*th character is *not* a space, we jump out of the loop. So if the IF statement has the form

IF condition THEN GOTO . . .

The condition used is

H$(j, z) <> " "

and as soon as the condition is found to be true, a jump out of the loop occurs, so that the last value assigned to *UPLen* is then the true unpadded length.

Here is the piece of program, written of course as a subroutine, so that we can insert a GO SUB in the main program exactly where we want.

```
600 REM SUB find UnPaddedLength of H$(j)
610 FOR z = STRLen TO 1 STEP -1
620 LET UPLen = z
630 IF H$(j, z) <> " " THEN GO TO 650
640 NEXT z
650 REM UPLen is now the UnPaddedLength of H$(j)
660 RETURN
670 REM *************************************
```

We have to make two small changes in the main program, in order to utlize this subroutine. The first is to change the PRINT statement that prints *H$(j)* so that it only prints the slice we want

```
530 PRINT H$(j, 1 TO UPLen)
```

but of course, immediately before that we need to call the new subroutine, in order to get the required value for *UPLen*

```
525 GO SUB 600
```

If you run the new version of this program the output shows a great improvement. However, there still remains one extremely unlovely feature. Wherever the end of a display line falls in the middle of a word, the word is split in two, part at the end of one line, the remainder at the beginning of the next line.

Putting newline into a string

It would be even better if we could include the ENTER token at an appropriate place between whole words in the strings concerned. The ENTER token, as you may have deduced, gets printed (displayed) as the signal for a newline. However, if you try to include it in a string, the computer thinks you are finished with entering that line. Furthermore, it will grumble because you seem to have left out the closing quote-mark of the string!

Now the ENTER token is stored in the computer like any other token, and has an integer code-value just as all the others have. If you look for ENTER in the table of code-values, you will see that its code-value is 13.

We can take advantage of this if we also take note of a very useful built-in function provided by the computer, called CHR$. This is itself a keyword. (It is the Extended mode character of the 'U' key.)

It works as follows. The expression

CHR$ n

gets evaluated as the *character* whose code value is *n*. So the value of CHR$ 13 is the ENTER keyword, which is the character for printing a newline. Following the usual style it is clearer to write in program

LET newline = 13

and when you want the newline character you can write CHR$ *newline* (which you can read as 'the character for newline').

Suppose we wanted to PRINT the string 'line 1 line 2', but with a newline character in the middle. You might try

PRINT "line 1 CHR$ newline line 2"

but that doesn't work because everyting inside the quote-marks is taken literally and actually gets printed as it stands. The solution is to use an expression consisting of three strings glued together, using a '+' sign as glue.

The two literal strings must be in quote-marks, but the middle one, the string expression, CHR$, is not.

Here is the revised instruction

PRINT "line 1" + CHR$ newline + "line 2"

Try it for yourself, and you will see that 'line 1' is displayed on one line, and 'line 2' on the next.

The house that Jack built

Now, to get back to our nursery rhyme, we can achieve a much neater effect if we use this treatment on the three longer strings in *H*$, namely *H*$(1) and *H*$(2) and *H*$(3).

But this program has now been modified and added to so many times that it is now the longest program we have built so far; so it is worth setting it out completely.

Notice that, although it is a comparatively large program, we have written it as three quite short subroutines, and a short main program, none of which are longer than 10 BASIC instructions. We never had to think about anything bigger than 10 lines.

Here is the program:

```
 80 REM House that Jack built program
 90 LET newline = 13
100 LET arraylen = 8
110 LET strlen = 44
120 DIM H$(arraylen, strlen)
130 GO SUB 300 :REM set up array H$
200 FOR k = 1 TO arraylen
210 GO SUB 500 :REM print kth verse
220 NEXT k
230 STOP
240 REM end of main program
250 REM ************************************************************
300 LET H$(1) = " the man all tattered and torn," + CHR$ newline + "who kissed"
310 LET H$(2) = " the maiden all forlorn," + CHR$(newline) + "who milked"
320 LET H$(3) = " the cow with the crumpled horn," +CHR$(newline) + "that tossed"
330 LET H$(4) = " the dog, that worried"
340 LET H$(5) = " the cat, that killed"
350 LET H$(6) = " the rat, that ate"
360 LET H$(7) = " the malt that lay in"
370 LET H$(8) = " the house that Jack built."
380 LET a$ = CHR$ newline + "This is"
390 RETURN
500 REM ************************************************************
505 REM print the kth verse SUB
510 PRINT a$
520 FOR j = arraylen + 1 - k TO arraylen
525 GO SUB 600 : REM find UnPaddedLen of h$(j)
530 PRINT H$(j, 1 TO UPLen)
540 NEXT j
545 PRINT
550 RETURN
560 REM ************************************************************
600 REM SUB find UnPaddedLength of H$(j)
610 FOR z = STRLen TO 1 STEP -1
620 LET UPLen = z
630 IF H$(j, z) <> " " THEN GO TO 650
640 NEXT z
650 REM UPLen is now the UnPaddedLength of h$(j)
660 RETURN
670 REM * The End *
680 REM ************************************************************
```

Actually, I haven't used the complete nursery rhyme. Why don't you try extending the program and modifying it, so that it will print the whole thing, using keen insertions of CHR$(13) to get a smart layout, like the one used in the final verse of the complete unabridged version which follows.

This is the horse
  and the hound and the horn,
That belonged to the farmer
  sowing his corn,
That kept the cock
  that crowed in the morn,
That waked the priest
  all shaven and shorn,
That married the man
  all tattered and torn,
That kissed the maiden
  all forlorn
That milked the cow
  with the crumpled horn,
That tossed the dog,
That worried the cat,
That killed the rat,
That ate the malt
That lay in the house
  that Jack built.

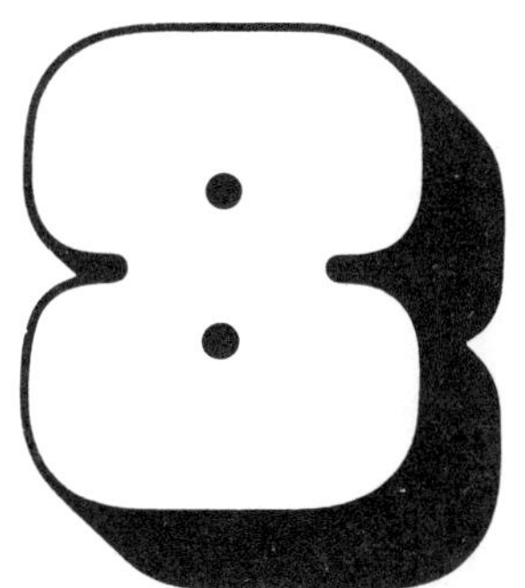

Hassles and hang-ups

Taking the hassle out of editing

A lot of time is spent editing programs, so it is worth learning how to make the system do the hard work for you.

There are certain basic operations you are constantly wanting to do.

(1) Delete a line
(2) Find a line
(3) Edit a line whose number you know

Deleting a line

This is simple. Just enter the line-number by itself. What happens is that you are entering an 'empty' line, and this replaces the one already there.

Using LIST

If you enter LIST, what happens? Try it and notice *exactly* what happens. The display starts with the lowest numbered line of program in store, and shows as much of it as will fit into the top 22 lines of the screen. If it won't all fit into 22 lines, a message appears on line 24 of the screen

scroll ?

(and the 23rd line is left blank)

You are expected to respond to the question 'scroll ?' by telling the computer either

Yes carry on listing

or

No, I've had enough

You can tell it 'no' by entering any one of four alternatives:

	n	
or	N	(i.e. CAPS SHIFT n)
or	SPACE	
or	BREAK	(i.e. CAPS SHIFT SPACE)

In each case, the upper 22 lines stay fixed, but the 24th line is replaced by the message

D BREAK – CONT repeats, Ø:1

This message may not look very helpful at first sight. It is there to tell you that you can carry on by entering any command you like. If you are so curious to find out what 'CONT repeats' means that you enter CONTINUE, you will find that line 24 goes blank, and the keyboard dies on you. The only way to bring it back to life is to enter BREAK again.

If you are trying to find a line somewhere near the end of a very long program, it can be very irritating having to scroll through several screens full of program which you don't want to see. One alternative is to enter

LIST n

where n is a line-number which comes before the line you are looking for, but is fairly near to it. In this case the display starts with line *n*.

When using LIST, you need to remember to enter N or SPACE as soon as you have found the place you want. If you forget, and enter some new command, or press the EDIT key, the scrolling simply continues, much to your irritation.

Finding the line you want without LIST

You can avoid the time-wasting use of LIST by moving the linecursor. The straightforward way of doing this is to press CAPS shift and 6 or 7 (6 for down and 7 for up). But this is equally tiresome because the cursor moves one line at a time and is very slow.

To move the cursor fast, you can enter a line-number which you know is not used in your program. This enters an empty line. Beware you don't accidentally delete a program line this way. Personally, I *never, never* use line-numbers ending in 9 in my programs. That way I know I can safely insert any line-number ending in 9 (with an empty line) just to move the linecursor.

Try this out. First press ENTER. You will get a display of a screenful of program which includes the line where the linecursor happens to be (even though you won't see the cursor displayed). If you now press EDIT, the line-cursor actually appears on the screen, against the first non-empty line with a line-number higher than the empty line you entered; and of course, the edit-line is brought down and copied into the editing area at the bottom of the screen. (If you don't want to change it just press ENTER.)

To move an instruction from line *p* to line *q*

Sometimes you want to keep an instruction unchanged, but move it to a different position in the program. To do this without having to type in the whole line, proceed as follows:

(1) Move the cursor to line *p* (by entering an empty line with number just below *p*, and ending in 9).
(2) Press the EDIT key.
(3) Delete the line number *p* and insert the value *q*. Then press ENTER.
(4) To delete the old line, just enter an empty line numbered *p*.

When LIST or ENTER gives you a blank screen

This is a trap you may fall into, after using instructions which change the colour of INK or PAPER, especially using random generation of colours in a program. Sometimes you may find that the program ends (or you press BREAK) at a time when PAPER and INK just happen to be the same colour!

It that is the case, when you press ENTER, nothing seems to happen, because the program is displayed with INK the same colour as PAPER. If you enter LIST, the result is similar, except that you may still get the message

scroll ?

because the colour setting instructions can't make INK and PAPER the same for the editing area. The computer is careful to ensure that in the part of the screen they always contrast, and so are always visible.

The quickest way to deal with this situation is to enter the direct command

PAPER 7 : INK Ø : BRIGHT 1 : CLS

Using bright 1 makes the screen whiter than white (just like you favourite washing powder), and makes reading the screen easier on the eyes. I use it all the time.

Some things to check when programs go wrong

There are two different kinds of situation when programming errors can hold you up.

(1) Watch your language – the computer may not like it! (You try to enter an instruction that looks perfectly OK, but the computer spits it back at you.) When you press ENTER, the line is not entered. Instead a flashing question-mark appears somewhere in the line. This means the computer objects either to the symbol before or the symbol after the question-mark.

Examples of things that can cause this are:

You typed in a keyword, letter by letter, instead of using the key-top token (like L,E,T instead of LET).

You didn't observe the rules of the BASIC language (like leaving out THEN in an IF. . . THEN instruction; or leaving out a closing quote-symbol).

You used more than one letter to name a loop control variable.

You assigned a string or character-type value (expression) to a numeric variable, or vice versa.

You used a semicolon instead of a colon to separate two BASIC instructions in the same line.

You used a colon to separate two items in a PRINT list, instead of comma or semicolon.

(2) With the second kind of error the program does not RUN properly. The instructions you entered were all accepted, but when you run the program, it stops with an error report.

There is a list of error reports in Appendix B (page 189) of the instruction manual that comes with the computer.

Any report starting with a number other than Ø or starting with a letter indicates that the computer found an error in you program while trying to run it. You can look up this error number (or letter) and find a little further information in Appendix B. Although that doesn't necessarily tell you *exactly* what is wrong, the error report is actually very useful. It has the general form:

Report-no. Message, Statement-no. :Substatement-no

For example, the following program is wrong

```
100  DIM x(4)
110  LET y = 53: LET x(5) = 8
```

and it stops with the report

3 Subscript wrong, 110:2

The most useful part of the report is the '110:2'. This means that the computer *detected* the error in line 110, in the second substatement in that line. It doesn't necessarily follow that the error is *there*, but that is where it was *detected* by the computer. In this example, the real error might be in line 100, which perhaps ought to be:

```
100  DIM x(40)
```

Whenever a subscript is wrong, there are always two possibilities. Either the subscript really is wrong, or it is correct and the DIM statement is wrong.

But with any error message, the important thing is to note the statement number and substatement number. You can rely on the the fact that the error occurs *in that statement or before it.* It doesn't occur after it.

In practice, errors are not always so obvious as in the example just given. But there is a lot of help available from the computer to find out what went wrong.

When the program stops, the computer still retains in its memory the values all the variables had at the time the program stopped. It can be very helpful to know what some of these values are, and you can find out by entering direct commands (without line-numbers) to make the computer PRINT them out.

For example, if the error was detected in a statement that is inside a loop, you can first find out how many times it went round the loop by printing the value of the loop control variable. Then you can print out the values of anything that seems relevant. It is step by step detective work; and you have to work backwards (through the program) from the point were the error was detected.

Another thing you can do is to insert PRINT instruction at critical points in the program to print out values which you think may be connected with what is going wrong, and run the program again.

Sometimes the program will run without an error report, but even so, you can tell it is wrong because it is not doing what you wanted it to do. The same techniques can be used to locate the part of the program where the error arises.

Using Cassette Tape

It is essential to save programs, or you have to type them in all over again, and it is possible to hit snags when you try to SAVE them, but following a few simple rules will help.

Rule 1

The success of the SAVE operation depends on you setting the volume control of your tape recorder at a suitable position. Too low gives a signal that is too weak. Too high gives so strong a signal that there is distortion. Either way, when you try to LOAD the program, the computer reports

R TAPE LOADING ERROR

A satisfactory setting for the volume control can be found only by trial and error. Start off with a half-way setting. Then try three-quarters, then try a quarter setting, and so on until you find approximately where the optimum position is.

Once you have found it, stick a piece of scotch tape over the control, to prevent it being accidentally moved any more.

Rule 2

The manual gives complicated rules about when it is OK to leave MIC and EAR jacks both plugged in to the tape recorder, and when you should pull one of them out.

I recommend the following simple rule which is easier to remember

NEVER leave both jacks plugged in at the same time

Plug in the MIC jack when you want to SAVE, and take it out when you have finished (to avoid writing to the tape by accident).

Plug in the EAR jack when you want to LOAD or VERIFY, and unplug it when you have finished.

Rule 3

As soon as you have SAVEd something, rewind the tape, change jack plugs (MIC out EAR in) and do a

VERIFY

This will immediately tell you whether the SAVE was successful. If it wasn't, you can try again, while the program you want to SAVE is still safely stored in computer memory.

Getting Organized

Once you have shown the tape recorder who is boss, by successfully doing a few SAVE, VERIFY, and LOAD operations, there is another worthwhile practice which is highly recommended. It is a way of dealing with the problem of knowing what is actually on which tape (after you have saved several modified versions of several programs on several tapes, or even in several places on the same tape – not recommended).

The trick is to voice-record on the tape at the beginning, using an external microphone plugged into the MIC sockets of the tape recorder. It is important to record the title under which the program has been SAVEd, and the *date.* The date is not important in itself, but is an excellent way of identifying each program so as to distinguish between different versions having the same title, without having to remember anything. If you are likely to SAVE several versions on the same day, add the time of day as well, for the same reason.

If you are acquainted with a friendly soldering iron

Here is a project which requires trivial effort and little financial outlay, but which greatly eases the burdens associated with SAVE, VERIFY and LOAD.

All you need is a small tin box, five-jack-sockets, and two small electrical switches of the size used on car dashboards. Once the box is made up, everything can be plugged into it and left plugged in. The box has two switches mounted in it. Each of them is a two-way switch. One is labelled SAVE/VERIFY or LOAD. The other is a MIC switch labelled VOICE/COMPUTER.

When you want to VERIFY or LOAD, you flick the first switch to the VERIFY or LOAD position. When you want to SAVE, you flick it to the other position, and also set the MIC switch to VOICE while you voice-dub the tape, and to COMPUTER while you SAVE the program. Nothing needs to be unplugged.

The first switch is a 2-position and 2-way switch. It has six terminals. The MIC switch is a simple 2-way switch with 3 terminals.

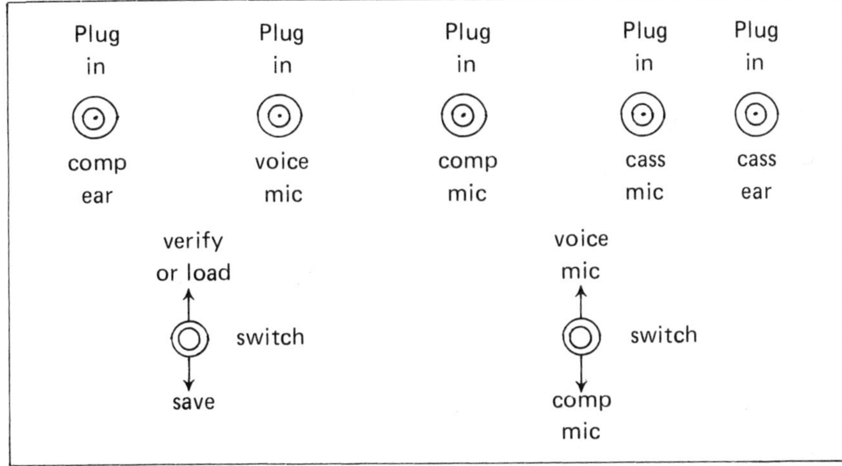

This is what the cassette manual control box looks like

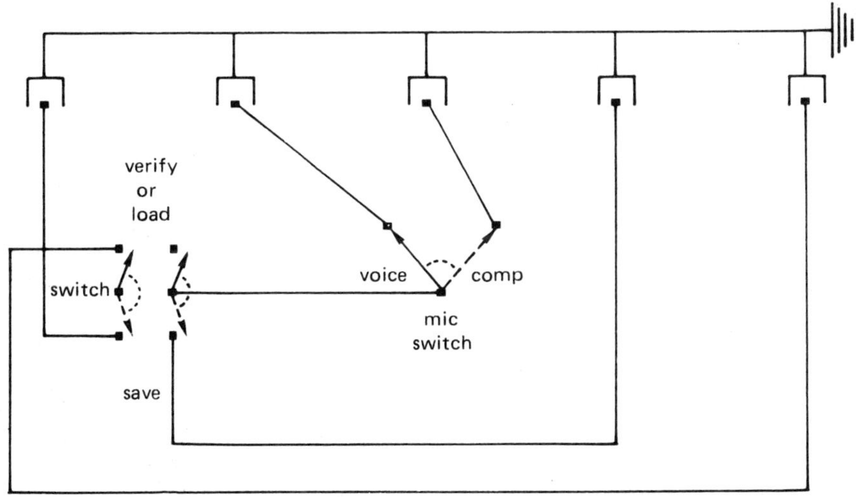

Wiring diagram for control box

Music micro please

The sounds emmitted by the computer are not particularly loud. But they are easy to control, and there are a number of interesting games we can play. This chapter will explain how to program the computer, not so much to be a musical instrument, but to be an aid to anyone who would like to use it to create simple musical compositions – and all without being able to read a note of music or know anything about musical theory.

It is easy to turn the typewriter keyboard into a musical keyboard, and we shall do that first. Then we shall see how to store tunes, play them back, or alter them by simple editing. It is also possible to get the computer to store rhythmic patterns – like dee-dah dee-dah dee-dah, or dah dee-dee dah dee-dee dah – you know the kind of thing; we can store waltz rhythms, tango rhythms, march rhythms – and then get the computer to play the tunes to different rhythms. The next thing we'll do is to get the computer to create new tunes from old ones, by making what are sometimes called transformations of them. A simple example of a transformation is to play a tune backwards. Adding a new rhythm after such a reversal produces quite a new melody; and there are some others.

The computer produces only one note at a time so you cannot get it to play chords. However, by playing all the notes of a chord in quick succession two or three times, you can get an effect rather like strumming a chord on a stringed instrument.

One way and another, this computer can be turned into quite a well-trained composer's aid. First let's see how to create a musical keyboard.

Using BEEP

The instruction that produces a musical note is called BEEP. The keyword BEEP must be followed by two numeric values, separated by a comma. The first is the duration in seconds of the note to be emitted, and then comes the so-called pitch of the note. The pitch is measured so that the note on a piano keyboard called middle C, (which you may like to think of as DOH in the tonic solfa) has a pitch equal to zero. The C that is one octave higher has pitch 12, and the C that is one octave lower has a negative pitch, minus 12. The notes in between are divided into 12 intervals, so that all the whole number (integer) values of pitch between Ø and 12 correspond to all the notes (including black and white ones) on a piano keyboard.

Thus

BEEP 1,Ø

produces a 'middle C' note lasting 1 second. The sequence of notes corresponding to the normal scale of C that you get on a piano by playing all the white notes in one octave, can be played on the computer by using the sequence of pitch values

Ø, 2, 4, 5, 7, 9, 11, 12

For those who can read music, this corresponds to the notes

C, D, E, F, G, A, E, C

So to play the scale of C on the computer we need to store these values in an array once and for all, so that any time we need it we can get the computer to look up the stored array values. (Adding a constant value to each value in the sequence gives you the scale in a new musical key.)

There is a way of storing a sequence of data values in a program which is very convenient to use when we know the values are going to be the same every time the program runs. If they are always the same, we don't want to have to input them more than once. Instead of using the instruction INPUT, which expects to find data entered from the keyboard, we use an instruction which starts witht he keyword READ. This expects to find its data in a list in another instruction which starts with the keyword DATA. A program can have as many DATA statements as you like, and they may occur anywhere in the program. When the program runs, they are ignored and by-passed, until the program gets to a READ statement. In a program with only one DATA statement, the READ statement takes the data items one at a time, in sequence, from that DATA statement. For example, to store the pitch values for the scale of C, we can write

```
100  DATA Ø, 2, 4, 5, 7, 9, 11, 12
110  DIM c(8) : RESTORE 100
120  FOR j = 1 TO 8
130  READ c(j)
140  NEXT j
```

and that will do it.

To play the scale of C, we use the values stored in the array c to give the pitch required, as follows

```
150  FOR j = 1 TO 8
160  BEEP Ø.2, c(j)
170  NEXT j
```

The sound produced by the built-in speaker is not very loud, but if you want it louder, just start your tape-recorder on record, before running the program. It will play back the tune much louder. (Of course, don't forget to plug the mic plug into the recorder first!)

To get a strumming effect, we need to store some more DATA, namely the sequence of pitch values that make up a pleasing harmonic set of notes to strum. The set that gives what musicians call a major chord, are: Ø, 4, 7, 12.

Now if a program has more than one DATA statement, then it is necessary to make sure that each READ statement in the program uses the correct DATA statement. This is done by using the RESTORE instruction, which restores the computer's internal place-marker for DATA statements to the line-number of the required DATA statement. Using this precaution, if we want to store the harmonic chord sequence of pitch values, we can write:

```
180  DIM h(4)
190  DATA Ø, 4, 7, 12
200  RESTORE 190
210  FOR j = 1 TO 4
220  READ h(j)
230  NEXT j
```

Now we have the stored values we can play an improved version of the C scale, using strumming instead of single notes. But, of course, first we need a subroutine to produce the strumming. We shall assume that a variable called *pitch* has been assigned the required value before the subroutine has been called. The subroutine can then be as follows:

```
1000 REM strum(pitch) SUBR
1010 FOR z = 1 TO 4
1020 BEEP 0.1, h(z) + pitch
1030 NEXT z
1040 RETURN
```

The improved version of the scale becomes:

```
250  FOR j = 1 TO 8
260  LET pitch = c(j): GOSUB 1000
270  NEXT j
```

Notice that in line 1020 of the *strum* subroutine, the value of the harmonic note was added to the value of the basic pitch to give the resultant *pitch* value used by BEEP. Actually this treatment works not only in the scale of C, but in all the other scales. If we want to change key and play the scale of A, or G, then we merely add the pitch difference (between A or G, and C) to the value of *pitch* before calling the strum subroutine. For example, the pitch of A is 9 HIGHER THAN C, so to play the scale of A, we could change line 160 to:

```
160  LET pitch = c(j) + 9 : GOSUB 1000
```

It is now time to open that musical keyboard, and here is how to do it.

Setting up the Musical Keyboard

We need yet another array of look-up values, this time for the whole keyboard. What we want to do is to associate the required pitch with each keytop. Now each keytop is a printable symbol (letter, digit, or keyword), which has its own numeric code inside the computer, between 1 and 255. There are 36 printable keytops, which gives 3 octaves (because 3 X 12 = 36). We can use, say, SYMBOL SHIFT to double this, and so get a note span of 6 octaves, which should be ample.

Of course, we don't know (without looking them up) the internal codes, but we always make the computer do this sort of chore. If we take the keytops in sequence, as they appear on the keyboard, in rows from top left to bottom right, we want the computer to associate pitch values (which increase by 1 each time in the same order) with the internal numeric code of the keytop symbol. For example, if the lowest pitch we want on our musical keyboard has the value *bottom,* then we want to store the value *bottom* as the element K(j) of our keyboard look-up array, where *j* has the value of CODE '1', because '1' is the keytop symbol of the key giving the lowest note.

```
LET K(CODE "1") = bottom
```

The next note up is to be associated with keytop '2' and must have a pitch of (*bottom* + 1), so we need

```
LET K(CODE "2") = bottom + 1
LET K(CODE "3") = bottom + 2
```

and so on, until the thirty-sixth key-top symbol, which is 'm', will need

```
LET K(CODE "m") = bottom + 35
```

The point of all this is so that, once all these are stored, if the musical keyboard is in use, then for any particular key pressed (and let us suppose that the character has been stored in *a*$), then the *pitch* required can be 'looked-up' by the computer when we tell it

```
LET pitch = K(CODE a$)
```

Just work through what happens when this is obeyed. Suppose the key-top character entered was 'q'. Now the internal code of 'q' happens to be 113, and so the pitch value stored for 'q' is stored in *K*(113), which is the same as *K*(CODE'q').

Now suppose we type in once and for all, a string which is a record of all the key-top symbols, in the same order as they occur on the keyboard. We can store this string in *s*$ by the instruction:

```
100  LET s$ = "1234567890qwertyuiopasdfghjklzxcvbnm"
```

The string *s*$ is 36 bytes in length, and by using the slicing technique, we can refer to each individual character in it. The first one, '1', is *s*$(1). The last one, 'm', is *s*$(36).
So to store the first 36 values of the *K* array we would write

```
105  LET bottom = -18
110  FOR j = 1 TO 36
120  LET j$ = s$(j)
130  LET K(CODE j$) = bottom + j - 1
140  NEXT j
```

In fact, we want to store 72 values, not 36, by using the whole set of keys together with SYMBOL SHIFT. It is desirable to get the same note from the same key-top, although 3 octaves higher when using SYMBOL SHIFT, rather than get a different note altogether; and we can arrange this by using a new string, and similar instructions, but adding exactly three octaves of pitch (that is the value 36) to the expression for pitch value that we store in the *K* array.

The new string is going to contain symbols that are printed as keywords, as well as single characters, but remember that they are still stored inside the computer as single bytes, using their code values.

```
200  LET t$ = "!@#$%&'( )_<=<>>= <> AND OR AT; " "STOP NOT STEP
TO THEN ↑-+=:£/*,."
210  FOR j = 1 TO 36
220  LET j$ = t$(j)
230  LET K(CODE j$) = (bottom +j-1) + 36
240  NEXT j
```

One important point to notice is that the quote symbol has been included in the string. This is done by including it twice in succession. Otherwise the computer would think it was merely marking the end of the string.

Of course, you might probably simplify line 230 to have the right-hand side read

bottom + j + 35

but the original is possibly clearer because you can see how it was derived.

However, we can simplify this program by combining the two strings into one that is 72 bytes long, and using only one loop:

```
 640>LET s$="1234567890qwertyuiopasdfghjklzxcvbnm"
:REM all the keytops in keyboard order
 650 LET s$=s$+"!@£$%&'()_<=<>>=<> AND  OR AT ;""
STOP NOT  STEP  TO  THEN ^-+=:`?/*,.":
 REM ditto with SYMBOL SHIFT
 660 LET bottom p=-18:     LET top p=bottom p+(LEN
s$-1)
 670 FOR j=1 TO LEN s$
 680 LET pitch=bottom p +j-1
 690 LET k(CODE s$(j))=pitch
 700 NEXT j
```

There are now 72 values entered at places which are scattered about in the array *K*, whose DIM statement was *K*(255), so most of the elements of *K* have not been used, and still have the value the computer starts them off with, which is zero. This could be a bit dangerous, because, we might, through a programming error (or some other accident) happen to have the computer look them up. To avoid this it is better to fill them all with some identical recognizable value, and have our program check every look-up to make sure we don't have a rogue value for *pitch.* A suitable value is one that is not a legal pitch, say 999, which is also highly recognizable. We can ensure that all the unused array elements are left with the value 999, by giving this value to *every* element *K*(1) to *K*(255) before we begin to store the wanted look-up values.

There is one more thing. When the musical keyboard is being used, there has to be some way of 'getting out of it', that is, getting the keyboard back into normal use, and we can use the keys for SPACE and ENTER as alternative ways of ending the use of the musical keyboard. We shall make provision for this by storing another arbitrary but impossible special value of *pitch* for each of these two keys. The negative value, –999 ? That will do nicely.

So, to tie up all the loose ends, here is a subroutine which sets up the musical keyboard, doing all the things that have just been discussed.

```
 610>REM ************ init muskey SUBR ***********
 620 DIM k(255)
 630 FOR j=1 TO 255: LET k(j)=999: NEXT j
 640 LET s$="1234567890qwertyuiopasdfghjklzxcvbnm"
: REM all the keytops in keyboard order
 650 LET s$=s$+"!@£$%&'()_<=<>>=<> AND  OR AT ;""
STOP NOT  STEP  TO  THEN ^-+=:`?/*,.":
 REM ditto with SYMBOL SHIFT
 660 LET bottom p=-18:    LET top p=bottom p+(LEN
s$-1)
 670 FOR j=1 TO LEN s$
 680 LET pitch=bottom p +j-1
 690 LET k(CODE s$(j))=pitch
 700 NEXT j
```

```
 710 LET k(13)=-999: LET k(32)=-999:    REM enter &
 space codes
 720 REM setup strum chords **********************
 730 DIM h(4)
 740 DATA 0,4,7,12
 750 RESTORE 0740
 760 FOR z=1 TO 4: READ h(z)
 770 NEXT z
 780 RETURN : REM ********** end of SUBR *********
```

How about USING the musical keyboard

We could now use the musical keyboard after a fashion by inputting a character and then using BEEP with the appropriate pitch found by computer look-up. But that would not be very much like a real keyboard, because each key would first have to be pressed, and then followed by ENTER.

There is another way of getting data from the keyboard directly a key is pressed, without using ENTER. To do this, you must not use the INPUT instruction. Instead, you use a special keyword called INKEY$. You will find this printed in green above the 'n' keytop. (To enter it you first press CAPS SHIFT & SYMBOL SHIFT both at the same time, which puts the keyboard in E-mode; then you press the n keytop, followed by ENTER).

If you use INKEY$ in an expression, its value is always the character-value in L-mode whose key is being pressed at the instant when the computer looks at INKEY$; that is, at the instant when it is obeying the instruction which uses it. If no key is being pressed at that instant, or if more than one key is being pressed at the same instant, then the value of INKEY$ is the empty string “ ”.

In order to make it possible to press one key after another, and use INKEY$ to get the value of the right key, a little care is needed in programming. After all, the computer only takes a tiny fraction of a second or so to look, while human fingers take at least a hundred times as long to keep a key pressed, and might easily press another key before the first is released.

So there has to be a tiny loop in which the computer looks at the keys over and over again (possibly hundreds of times) until something happens.

The first thing to make sure of is that the computer doesn't try to read the same key more than once. This can easily happen if it looks again in a few hundredths of a second. We can make sure of this by making a little loop that waits until nothing is being pressed:

```
10   REM wait until all fingers OFF
20   IF INKEY$ <> " " THEN GO TO 20
```

Line 20 will be repeated over and over again until INKEY$ has the value of the empty string, meaning no keys are being pressed. But as soon as all fingers (and elbows) are OFF the keyboard, INKEY$ will have the value “ ”, the empty string, and the program will stop looping around the line 20 and carry on to the next instruction.

The next thing required is that the computer again looks at the keys over and over again, but this time it is waiting to find that a key *has* been pressed. This requires a very similar loop to the previous one, but with one essential difference:

```
30   REM wait until ONE finger ON
40   IF INKEY$ = " " THEN GO TO 40
```

This instruction tells the computer to look again if it found the empty string. It stops looping as soon as INKEY$ has a non-empty value.

You can put these two loops together, follow them with a PRINT INKEY$ instruction, and follow that with GO TO back to the beginning to wait for the next character:

```
10   REM wait until FINGERS OFF
20   IF INKEY$ <> "  " THEN GO TO 20
30   REM wait until FINGER ON
40   IF INKEY$ = " " THEN GO TO 40
50   PRINT INKEY$
70   GO TO 20
```

Try this out, and you will see that it makes the computer behave rather like a typewriter. Of course, this program never ends; it just sits there and loops round waiting for keys to be pressed. In order to escape from it, you have to press CAPS SHIFT and BREAK at the same time, which BREAKS into the program completely.

The invisible empty string

When I was very young, a favourite rhyme I learned, went:

> *The other day, upon the stair*
> *I saw a man who wasn't there.*
> *He wasn't there again today –*
> *I wish that man would go away!*

The empty string strongly reminds me of that man. It crops up everywhere! And most of the time, no-one can see it. But we have ways of making it seen!

Take the little INKEY$ program we have just been looking at, and change line 50 to

```
50   PRINT CODE INKEY$
```

The computer still behaves like a typewriter when the modified program is RUN, but instead of printing the *character* corresponding to the key you press, it prints that character's CODE-value.

According to the list of code values printed on page 183 of the Sinclair programming manual, the code value Ø is not used. Actually this is not true, and you should amend your manual to show it.

The value Ø is the CODE value of the empty string.

You can demonstrate this by running the program and continually pressing two keys at once. Quite frequently, the value Ø will get printed.

This demonstrates two things. The first is that Ø is the CODE value of the empty string, the second is that, surprisingly, this program is not as good as it first seemed to be. It seemed to be cleverly designed to *avoid* getting the empty string printed. Line 40 waits until the empty string has *gone away* before going on to line 50 when something is printed. It *doesn't actually work because the value of INKEY$ can change* between the time when line 40 is obeyed and the time when line 50 is obeyed, especially if you are pressing two keys at once, either purposely or accidentally, or even if you are merely hitting two keys in quick succession.

In our music program, *we shall want to use the CODE-value of the character keyed in* as the *subscript* of an array. In this case, the value Ø will be illegal when used as a subscript, and will make our program crash.

However, we can deal with the problem of INKEY$ changing its value. All we have to do is freeze its value by *storing* it in a character variable *c*$. After that we can refer to that variable, which doesn't keep changing like INKEY$ does.

Here is the revised 'bomb-proof' version:

```
10   REM wait until fingerS OFF
20   LET c$ = INKEY$ : REM value frozen !
30   IF c$ <> "" THEN GO TO 20
40   REM wait till ONE finger ON
50   LET c$ = INKEY$ : REM new value frozen !
60   IF c$ = "" THEN GO TO 50
70   PRINT CODE c$
100  GO TO 10
```

If you run this, it seems OK at first – no zeros get printed. But there is still a way of crashing this program which you may discover.

When the screen gets filled with print lines, the usual message

"SCROLL ? "

comes up at the bottom of the screen. When the computer asks 'SCROLL?', pressing almost any key will cause scrolling to continue, so the program carries on. But not every key! If you press 'n' or SPACE or STOP, the program is interrupted completely, and the computer reports at the bottom of the screen

D BREAK – CONT repeats

It would be desirable to prevent the 'SCROLL?' enquiry from appearing, since it is likely to be a nuisance; and this is quite easy to do. The computer keeps a count of the number of lines to be printed before it makes each 'SCROLL?' enquiry. It keeps this count in a memory location not normally used by your BASIC program, and the action you can take is to alter the count in that store location so that it never gets counted down to zero. But how can that be done?

The POKE instruction

This instruction takes the form

POKE address, value

where 'address' is an expression which gives the address whose contents you want to change, and 'value' is another expression which gives the value you want to poke into that address.

So the POKE instruction is quite easy to use, but before it can be effectively used, you need to know something about which addresses the system uses for what purposes. There is a list of these addresses (called 'System variables') starting on page 173 of the Sinclair Programming Manual. One of them, called SCR CT (for scroll count) is listed on page 175, and its address is 23692. In fact, the explanatory note listed with SCR CT tells you what to do:

POKE 23692, 255

So if we insert two more lines in the INKEY program, it will be as bomb-proof as any program can be:

```
80   REM avoid "SCROLL?" message
90   POKE 23692, 255
```

Try running the final version, and you will find you can press as many keys at once as you like, but try as you may, you cannot now crash this program. You can of course, bring it to a halt, as you can *ANY* program whatever (*except* when it is expecting INPUT data), by pressing CAPS SHIFT and BREAK. (This is what those keys are intended for.)

For a text-inputting program, this little program would now be most useful. However, if we are not going to run into SCROLLING problems, we can forget about the last modification, at least for the time being.

Another useful POKE is one that makes any key 'tink' merrily when you press it down if it actually registers. You may already have noticed that, sometimes, when you press a key, it fails to register, possibly resulting in error and irritation. To make the keys 'tink', you need to POKE a value into another system variable. The instruction to do this is

POKE 23609, 30

After that, the keys will 'tink' when INPUT is being used (though not for INKEY$).

Coming back to our musical keyboard, now that we have toughened it up, we do need to have a way of escaping from it and going to some other part of our main BASIC program instead of stopping the program dead in its tracks by using BREAK.

To provide a more elegant exit, so that the program may go into this sequence and come out without ending the program, we can insert a test to see if a key has been pressed which we dont't otherwise want to use in the program.

In the musical keyboard program, both the ENTER key and the SPACE key were saved for precisely this purpose, and were given stored values of minus 999.

Adapting the INKEY$ program to the form of a subroutine which we can exit without crashing the program, and which is suitable for using to play our musical keyboard any time we want it (once it has been set up) we can use the following:

```
 790>REM ********** play-keyboard SUBR ***********
 800 CLS : PRINT "The keyboard"'"is now a musical
keyboard."'"Start Playing !"'''"The  SPACE  key ca
n be used to"'"indicate a (silent) pause."'''"When
 you have picked out a tune you want to store, wri
te it downbefore you return to the"'"TUNES Menu."'
''"To return to  menu, hit ENTER."
 810 REM wait till NO finger ON
 820 LET c$=INKEY$
 830 IF c$<>"" THEN  GO TO 0820
 840 REM wait till ONE finger ON
 850 LET c$=INKEY$
 860 IF c$="" THEN  GO TO 0850
 870 IF c$=CHR$ 13 THEN  GO TO 0930
 880 IF c$=" " THEN  GO TO 820
 890 LET pitch=k(CODE c$)
 900 LET duration=1
 910 GO SUB 950: REM strum
 920 GO TO 820
 930 RETURN : REM ****** end of subroutine *******
```

```
940 REM *********** strum SUBRoutine ************
950 FOR d=1 TO duration
960 FOR Y=1 TO 4: BEEP .02,h(Y)+pitch: NEXT Y
970 NEXT d
980 RETURN : REM ********************************
```

A complete program to use these subroutines needs in addition subroutines which set up the values for the scale of C, and the values for the harmonic chords, which have been described in detail in the preceding pages.

So far, of course, we can't produce real music, only sequences of notes, all the same length. Real music will come later. But we *can* pick out the melodies we want on the strings, so that we can play them without error when we want to store them in the computer.

How to store melodies

How to organize the data

Before anything else, we need to plan a way in which the tune can be *represented* in the computer memory. Now, our starting point is the fact that the tune is entered as a string of bytes, and therefore that is a convenient way to store it. But we probably shall want to be able to store a number of different tunes. Each one of these is representable as a string of bytes, but each of different (unforeseeable) length. In addition, we need to be able to refer to each tune, preferably by a name supplied when the tune is stored.

So we have the following *elements* of *information* for *each tune* we store in computer memory

	information	type of data
(1)	name of tune	short string of limited length
(2)	tune itself	string of variable length
(3)	length of tune	numeric (number of bytes)

We can think of the information about each tune as a collection of different pieces of data, each telling something important about the way the tune is to be stored; and we shall need this information in order to be able to *retrieve* the tune when we want to hear it again, alter it, or use it in any way.

Each time we store a tune, we also have to store its name and its length. It can be quite helpful to use a diagram to represent the data we want to store for each tune, extending and adding detail to the notes about it above:

NAME	LENGTH	TUNE
name of tune. can be a character string of up to say 24 bytes	number of bytes in the string representing the tune itself	a character string whose length is anything from 1 (byte) upwards. (The tune itself.)

We can think of this as a complete record of all we need to know about each string. But we might want to store up to say 10 tunes. If so, then we shall need 10 of these records. But in each record there is a big difference between NAME and LENGTH on the one hand, and the TUNE on the other. This is because every NAME can be given the same storage space and every LENGTH can too. But for each TUNE, the space needed is unpredictable and varies from tune to tune.

Thus we can easily use an array with one element for each name, say

```
DIM n$(10, 24)
```

giving 10 strings each 24 bytes long for storing names, and another array with an element for each length, say

```
DIM l(10)
```

But the best thing to do with the tunes themselves is to pack them into a single character variable, say *m$*, because, unlike an array, its length is variable and we can store the tunes one after another, using the string-glueing operator '+' to do it. As we intend keeping a record of name and length, it will be easy to get the tune we want out of *m$* by using slicing.

We also need to keep a record of the number of tunes that have been stored, so that we can add 1 to it each time a tune is stored, and we can use a variable called *no of tunes* to do this.

For example, we start off by doing this after the necessary DIM statements for name and length: This piece of program doesn't actually *do* anything, it is merely a piece of necessary organization of the data

```
100  LET max = 10
110  DIM n$(max, 24)
120  DIM l(max)
130  LET no of tunes = 0
140  LET m$ = " "
```

Notice that we started off *m$* as the empty string. This was so that we can glue strings on to it every time a tune is stored, including the first time. You can't glue a string on to another string that isn't there, but you *can glue a* string on to an empty string. An empty string is like an empty box. That's quite different from a box that isn't there.

We shall assume the program gets the user to input each tune into a variable *a$* and its name into another variable *b$*. Then it has to work out where to store them permanently. And that's actually terribly easy:

```
100  LET m$ = m$ + a$
110  LET no of tunes = no of tunes + 1
130  LET n$(no of tunes) = b$
140  LET l(no of tunes) = LEN a$
```

The program can do exactly the same four instructions unaltered, every time a new tune is to be stored. The first instruction glues the tune on to the end of *m$*. The second updates the number of tunes, by adding 1. The third stores the name, and the fourth stores the length.

However, someone might try to store more than 10 tunes. If so the program will crash. It's no good just increasing the value 10. However high you put it, someone will crash it. Put it higher if you like (by increasing *max*) but to prevent the possibility of the program crashing, it should test *no of tunes* to make sure it doesn't exceed *max*. A simple check would be made by inserting the extra line

```
120  IF no of tunes > max THEN PRINT "Too many tunes" : STOP
```

Let us try to get a picture of what the tune data look like in store when several tunes have been stored. Suppose that three tunes have been stored. The first, called 'Mary' is 23 bytes long; the second, called 'She loves me' is 47 bytes long; and the third, called 'Don't say no' is 35 bytes long. A map of the store could be represented like this:

no of tune	NAME		LENGTH		TUNE
	Index of n$ array	n$ array	Index of l array	l array	m$
1	1	the name "Mary" is stored in n$(1)	1	23 is stored in l(1)	the tune called "Mary" is stored in m$(1 TO 23)
2	2	the name "she loves me" is stored in n$(2)	2	47 is stored in l(2)	the tune called "she loves me" is stored in m$(24 TO 70)
3	3	the name "don't say no" is stored in n$(3)	3	35 is stored in l(3)	the tune called "don't say no" is stored in m$(71 TO 105)

A subroutine for storing tunes can be written as follows:

```
 990>REM ************ store tune SUBR ***********
1000 INPUT "Enter token string "'"of tune to be st
ored."'"If no tune to store, hit ENTER   ",a$
1010 IF a$="" THEN  RETURN
1030 IF no of tunes=max THEN  PRINT "Sorry, too ma
ny tunes."''"enter CONT to continue": STOP : RETUR
N
1040 INPUT "Enter name of new tune."'"If no tune t
o store, hit ENTER   ",b$
1050 IF b$="" THEN  RETURN
1060 LET no of tunes=no of tunes+1
1070 LET m$=m$+a$
1080 LET n$(no of tunes)=b$
1090 LET l(no of tunes)=LEN a$
1100 RETURN : REM ********* end of SUBr **********
```

Suppose there are a few more tunes stored, and we now want to actually find one that we have previously stored. How do we do it?

Whistling up a tune from store

We shall assume the program has asked the user to input the name of the wanted tune, and this name is input into the string variable *b*$.

Firstly the program has to find which element of *n*$ contains the same string as *a*$. We shall look at exactly how in more detail a little later. For the moment, we shall suppose that the program finds the value of *k* for which *n*$(*k*) = *b*$. We have found the name. Now to find the tune itself. This is stored in *m*$, and we can now work out exactly where by adding together the lengths of all the tunes that come in front of it. This addition can be done in the same loop that checks the names stored until it finds the one we want. We can get the computer to look at every name, that is every element of *n*$, from *n*$(1) to *n*$(*no of tunes*), and at every length from *l*(1) to *l*(*no of tunes*). So our program will be something like this:

```
100  LET start = 1
110  FOR j = 1 TO no of tunes
120  IF n$(j) = b$ THEN LET wanted = j: GO TO 160
130  LET start = start + l(j) − 1
140  NEXT j
150  PRINT "NOTHING STORED WITH NAME", b$: STOP
160  PRINT m$(start TO l(wanted) − 1)
170  STOP
```

Notice that line 120 ensures that the program jumps out of the loop as soon as the wanted name has been found. Only if the wanted name is not found at all is the loop completed for all values. In this case, the program arrives at line 150, informs the user, and stops. If, however, the name was found, the jump goes right over line 150 to line 160, which prints out the actual string that representes the tune, and then stops.

So far, so good. This program looks fine. Going over it carefully, it seems to be logically sound. Unfortunately, it doesn't work. You can try it out, by using it in conjunction with the *store tune* subroutine. First store a couple of tunes. Then, give *b*$ the value of one of the names you know you have stored, say 'Alice'. Surprise, surprise, the computer comes up with

"nothing stored with name. alice"

So you get the computer to print out the names it does have stored. And there among them is

"alice"

There is a simple explanation to this teaser. The fault is in the line

```
120  IF n$(j) = b$ THEN LET wanted = j: GO TO 160
```

Remember that *n*$ was defined by a DIM statement

```
LET max = 10
DIM n$(max, 24)
```

which means that *n*$ in an array of 10 strings, each of them 24 characters long.

When 'alice' is stored in *n*$(*j*), the computer pads out this short string of only 4 letters, by adding 19 spaces on to the end of it. So *n*$(*j*) is a 24-character string.

Later, when looking for 'alice', the program above asks the computer to compare the 24-character string in *n*$(*j*) (that is, 'alice   ', notice the 10 spaces), with the 5-character string in *b*$ (that is, 'alice', no spaces). Naturally the computer finds they are not the same.

So we have to be careful to ask it to compare strings of the same length. Using slicing, this is easy, and we can change line 120 to read

```
120  IF n$(j, 1 TO LEN b$) = b$ THEN LET wanted = j : GO TO 160
```

and this time it works.

Alternatively, we can pad out *b*$ to the full length of *b*$(*j*) before asking the computer to compare it:

```
FOR z = LEN b$ + 1 TO 24
LET b$ = b$ + " "
NEXT z
```

If we do that before the comparison loop begins, then everything will be OK.

Now that we have sketched the skeleton of what is required, we can expand it, as usual into a subroutine, complete with knobs and whistles (which is appropriate for whistling up a tune). In the subroutine, in addition to printing the tune, we shall store it temporarily in *a*$, in case we want to do anything else with it while we have it handy. So, on return from the subroutine,

a$ will have the tune
start will have its starting point in *m*$
wanted will have its tune number, or index in the arrays *l* and *n*$.

That way the program is all set to do anything else that's required with that tune.

```
1110>REM ************* get tune SUBr *************
1120 INPUT " Enter name of tune wanted","or else j
ust hit ENTER",b$
1130 IF b$="" THEN  RETURN
1140 LET start=1
1150 FOR z=LEN b$+1 TO 15: LET b$=b$+" ": NEXT z
1160 FOR z=1 TO no of tunes
1170 IF n$(z)=b$ THEN  LET wanted=z: GO TO 1260
1180 LET start=start+l(z)
1190 NEXT z
```

Listing continued next page

```
1200 CLS : PRINT b$,"    not found"'"***************
*****************************************************
"
1210 PRINT "Full list of names stored is"''
1220 FOR z=1 TO no of tunes
1230 PRINT n$(z),l(z);" notes long"
1240 NEXT z: PRINT
1250 GO TO 1120
1260 REM name found
1270 LET a$=m$(start TO start+l(wanted)-1)
1280 PRINT b$,"found"'a$:  RETURN : REM end of get
 tune SUB*********************************
```

One of the most likely times we should want to use *get tune* is when we want to play it over again and listen to it. A subroutine *replay tune* is fairly straightforward now that we already have *get tune*:

```
1290>REM ************ replay tune SUBr ***********
1300 GO SUB 1120: REM get tune
1310 IF b$="" THEN  RETURN
1320 FOR z=1 TO LEN a$
1330 LET pitch=k(CODE a$(z))
1340 LET duration=0.35
1350 BEEP duration,pitch
1360 NEXT z
1370 GO TO 1300
1380 RETURN : REM *** end of replay tune SUBr ****
```

Notice that Line 1310, together with line 1130, provides a non-irritating escape for the user who suddenly decides to change his or her mind about wanting a tune. RETURN will take him back to where he was in the first place.

Line 1330 uses the look-up table in the array *k*( ) that was set up when we created the musical keyboard, in Chapter 8, (initialize musical keyboard SUBr).

Simple text-editing – (or striking a wrong note)

Having stored a melody, and got it back to look at it and listen to it, you might want to change it. Since the melody is really just a string, a subroutine to edit it may be quite useful, not only in this music program, but also for some other program, concerned with text processing (which is what this chapter is really all about).

The most general and useful operation to have for editing text of any kind is one which allows you to replace a substring by a new substring. The same operation can be used for *deletion* of a substring. All you do then is replace the unwanted substring by the empty string.

To organize replacement of one substring by another, it is convenient to think of the whole original string as consisting of three parts:

head,
middle,
tail,

the middle being the part we want to replace. (If the part we want to replace happens to be right at the beginning, we can still think of it as the middle, provided we regard the head as the empty string. Similarly, if the part to be replaced is right at the end, we can still regard it as the middle provided we take the tail to be the empty string.)

Text-editing is of widespread and general use, but we shall think of it here as editing a TUNE. Then we can build a subroutine, *alter tune,* which starts by calling *get tune.* That way, we can assume that:

(1) the text to be edited is in *m*\$ beginning at *m*\$(*start*)
(2) its length is in *l*(*wanted*)

Let us assume the substring we want to replace in this text is *o*\$. First we'll store the length of *o*\$ in *olen*. The next thing to do is to locate *o*\$ in *m*\$. So we want to examine each substring of the same length as *o*\$ in *m*\$, starting at *m*\$(*start*) and carrying on until the number of tokens left is 1 less than *olen*. So the loop we use needs to be

```
FOR z = start TO (start + l(wanted) – olen)
```

The expression for the final value of the loop control variable *z*, is a bit tricky. The last byte of the text we are concerned with is *m*\$(*start* + *l*(*wanted*) – 1). The last byte of it that can possibly be the *first* byte of a substring whose length is *olen*, is (*olen* – 1) bytes before that. Subtracting (*olen* – 1) from (*start* + *l*(*wanted*) – 1) gives us (*start* + *l*(*wanted*) – *olen*).

If you don't follow this piece of arithmetic, draw a line of boxes to represent the text, and label each with the value of its index (subscript). Use *actual* numbers and an actual string and substring, and check that the expressions given are correct.

Every time we go through this loop we are going to test whether the current value of *z* is the one we *want,* that is, is it the beginning of a substring that matches *o*\$? If it is, we shall jump out of the loop, having found what we are looking for. If we reach the end of the loop without jumping out, it means that a matching string was *not* found, because it wasn't there. So far then, we shall have, inside the loop, something like

```
LET w = z
IF o$ = m$(z TO z + olen – 1) THEN GOTO found
```

Immediately after the end of the loop, we'll need to deal with the fact that the substring *o*\$ was not found. The best thing to do is to let the user know this and 'have another try' at entering *o*\$.

But if *o*\$ has been matched, we jump out of the loop *past* this and tackle the job of changing *o*\$ for a new substring *c*\$. We have the position in *m*\$ of the first byte of *o*\$, because we stored it in *w*. So we shall use this to find the *head* of our text. The new middle will be *c*\$, and we shall also have to glue on the tail. We shall use *h*\$ for the head and *t*\$ for the tail, using

LET h\$ = m\$(start TO w − 1)
LET t\$ = m\$(start + l(w) TO LEN m\$)

Notice that the tail includes not only the rest of our particular TUNE, but also all the other TUNES following it, stored in *m*\$. The final job we have to do is to update the stored value of the length of the altered TUNE, in *l*(*wanted*).

Here is the complete subroutine:

```
1390>REM ************ alter tune SUBr ************
1400 GO SUB 1120: REM get tune
1410 IF b$="" THEN  RETURN
1420 INPUT "Enter string to be changed."'"If nothi
ng to change, hit ENTER",o$
1430 IF o$="" THEN  RETURN
1440 LET olen=LEN o$
1460 FOR z=start TO start+l(wanted)-olen
1470 LET w=z
1480 IF o$=m$(w TO w+olen-1) THEN  GO TO 1520: REM
 name found
1490 NEXT z
1500 PRINT o$'"not found"
1510 INPUT "string not found"'"Hit ENTER and try a
gain",q$

1515 GO TO 1420
1520 INPUT "Enter fresh string"'"or hit ENTER to d
elete"'f$
1530 LET t$=m$(start+l(wanted) TO LEN m$): REM tai
l of unaltered tunes stored after in m$
1540 LET h$=m$(start TO w-1)
1550 LET a$=h$+f$+m$(w+olen TO start+l(wanted)-1):
 PRINT ''"Tune is now"''a$
1560 LET m$=m$(1 TO start-1)+a$+t$
1570 LET l(wanted)=l(wanted)+LEN f$-olen: REM new
length of tune stored
1580 GO TO 1420
1590 RETURN : REM **** end of alter tune SUBr ****
```

Line 1580 sends the computer back to the beginning, in case the user wants to change more than one substring in the same TUNE. When the user has finished editing, and the computer is sent back to line 1420 again, he just hits ENTER, which stores the empty string in *o*$. In that case, line 1430 returns the computer to the part of the program from which the subroutine was called.

11

Modifying programs — I got rhythm

We now have four subroutines, *store tune, get tune, alter tune, play tune.* We shall want four extremely similar subroutines which do similar tasks but work on the strings which represent rhythms instead of tunes.

It would be pointless to start all over again and do, over again, all the work put into designing and running such similar programs.

In some other languages, but not BASIC, it is easy to get the same subroutine to process different data, provided the new data has the same structure. We shall discuss this further in Chapter 18. In the meantime, we'll look at how to modify programs in a systematic way.

How to make systematic changes

It is very difficult to do this without a print-out of the program you want to modify. A print-out can be clearly marked up, with all the intended changes, before sitting down to the keyboard. Otherwise, you will be jumping backwards and forwards over the program instead of working steadily through it, when you actually make the changes. If you have no printer, the next best thing is to make carefully a systematic list of all the changes, and when that is complete, re-write it in line-number order.

We can start to build our list of systematic changes something like this:

(1) change every occurrence of 'tune' to 'rhythm'
(2) change every occurrence of 'TUNE' to 'RHYTHM'

The next obvious step is to introduce new variables for the storage of the rhythm strings, their names, and their lengths:

(3) change every '*m*$' to '*r*$', (rhythm strings)
(4) change every '*n*$' to '*i*$', (identifiers)
(5) change every '*l*(' to '*s*(', (size)

a$, *b*$, are used only for temporary storage of the string and its name, so they do not need to be changed.

And that is the end of the list of systematic changes. To convert this into the second list, we go through it and note the line-numbers affected by each systematic change. Then we can go to the computer, and, starting with a copy of the original subroutines, we can edit the affected lines in line-number order, ticking off each one on the list as we do it.

There is one modification that is advisable, which helps to prevent the program from crashing as a consequence of storing strings which are invalid for rhythms. Every character in a rhythm string should be a digit, ('1' to '9'). (It is easy to include a value for 10 by using the character whose CODE value is 1 greater than the CODEvalue of '9'. Looking up the CODE-value table, we can see this is colon, ':'.) The modification suggested is that the *store rhythms* SUBroutine should check that the character-string entered for storage as a rhythm contains only valid characters. This did not arise with *store tune,* because every character on the keyboard is valid in a TUNE string.

To do the checking, we can set up a string of all the valid characters, say

```
LET x$ = "123456789:"
```

and loop through them for every character of *a*\$. This means we need two loops, one inside the other. The outside loop is to loop through the *a*\$ characters. The inside loop is to loop through the *x*\$ characters comparing each one with the current character of *a*\$:

```
971 FOR z = 1 TO LEN a$
972 FOR y = 1 TO LEN x$
973 IF a$(z) = x$(y) THEN GO TO 977 :REM next z
974 NEXT y
975 PRINT "Your rhythm string contains invalid characters. "'"The valid characters are"'x$
976 GO TO 950 :REM re-input rhythm string
977 NEXT z
```

As soon as each character of *a*\$ is found to match one of *x*\$, there is a jump out of the inner, checking loop to the NEXT z line (977). If the inner loop gets completed without such a match being found, there was an invalid character. So a message to that effect is printed and there is a jump back to the line where the string was input, so that the user can try again.

The line-numbers used above are chosen so that these lines could be squeezed in between line 960 and 970 in the *store tune* SUBroutine.

But, now that we have completed our modifications and produced our new rhythm-handling subroutines by working on the old, tune-handling subroutines, we need to completely re-number all the lines, before we can actually include the new subroutines in the same program as the old ones.

This again requires some care, because, as a result of renumbering the lines, the line-numbers used in GO TO statements have to be changed as well.

A complete version of the new subroutines, after renumbering, is as follows:

```
2900>REM *********** store rhythm SUBr ***********
2910 LET x$="123456789"
2920 INPUT "Enter token string "'"of rhythm to be
stored."'"If no rhythm to store, hit ENTER    ",a$
2930 IF a$="" THEN  RETURN
2940 FOR z=1 TO LEN a$: FOR y=1 TO LEN x$
2950 IF a$(z)=x$(y) THEN  GO TO 2980
2960 NEXT y
2970 PRINT "Your RHYTHM STRING contains invalid to
kens."'"The valid tokens are"'"        ";x$: GO TO 29
20
2980 NEXT z
2990 INPUT "Enter name of rhythm.    ",b$
3000 LET no of rhythms=no of rhythms+1
```

```
3010 IF no of rhythms>max THEN  PRINT ''"Sorry, to
o many rhythms.": LET no of rhythms=no of rhythms-
1: PRINT ''"enter CONT to continue": STOP : RETURN

3020 LET r$=r$+a$
3030 LET i$(no of rhythms)=b$
3040 LET s(no of rhythms)=LEN a$
3050 RETURN : REM ********** end of SUBr *********


3060 REM *********** get rhythm SUBr *************
3070 INPUT "Enter name of rhythm wanted","or else
just hit ENTER",b$
3080 IF b$="" THEN  RETURN
3090 LET start=1
3100 FOR z=LEN b$+1 TO 15: LET b$=b$+" ": NEXT z
3110 FOR z=1 TO no of rhythms
3120 IF i$(z)=b$ THEN  LET wanted=z: GO TO 3210
3130 LET start=start+s(z)
3140 NEXT z
3150 CLS : PRINT b$,"   not found"'"**************
**************************************************
"
3160 PRINT "Full list of names stored is"''
3170 FOR z=1 TO no of rhythms
3180 PRINT i$(z),s(z);" notes long"
3190 NEXT z: PRINT
3200 GO TO 3070
3210 REM name found
3220 LET a$=r$(start TO start+s(wanted)-1)
3230 PRINT b$,"found"'a$: RETURN :
 REM *********** end of get rhythm SUBr **********

3240>REM ******** replay rhythm SUBr ************
3250 GO SUB 3070: REM get rhythm
3260 IF b$="" THEN  RETURN
```

Listing continued next page

```
3270 FOR z=1 TO LEN a$
3280 LET duration=0.1*(CODE a$(z)-CODE ("0"))
3290 BEEP duration,0
3300 NEXT z
3310 RETURN : REM ** end of replay rhythm SUBr ***
```

```
3320 REM ***** alter rhythm SUBr *****************
3325 LET x$="123456789:"
3330 GO SUB 3070: REM get rhythm
3340 IF b$="" THEN  RETURN
3350 INPUT "Enter string to be changed."'"If nothi
ng to change, hit ENTER",o$
3360 IF o$="" THEN  RETURN
3370 LET olen=LEN o$
3390 FOR z=start TO start+s(wanted)-olen
3400 LET w=z
3410 IF o$=r$(w TO w+olen-1) THEN  GO TO 3450: REM
 string found
3420 NEXT z
3430 PRINT o$'"not found"
3440 INPUT "string not found"'"Hit ENTER and try a
gain",q$: GO TO 3350
3450 INPUT "Enter fresh string"'"or hit ENTER to d
elete"'f$
3452 FOR z=1 TO LEN a$: FOR y=1 TO LEN x$
3454 IF a$(z)=x$(y) THEN  GO TO 3460
3456 NEXT y
3458 PRINT "Your fresh string contains invalid tok
ens."'"The valid tokens are"'"     ";x$: GO TO 345
0
3460 NEXT z
3465 LET t$=r$(start+s(wanted) TO LEN r$): REM tai
l of unaltered rhythms stored after in r$
3470 LET h$=r$(start TO w-1)
```

```
3480 LET a$=h$+f$+r$(w+olen TO start+s(wanted)-1):
 PRINT ''"Tune is now"''a$
3490 LET r$=r$(1 TO start-1)+a$+t$
3500 LET s(wanted)=s(wanted)+LEN f$-olen: REM new
length of rhythm stored
3510 GO TO 3350
3520 RETURN : REM *** end of alter rhythm SUBR ***
```

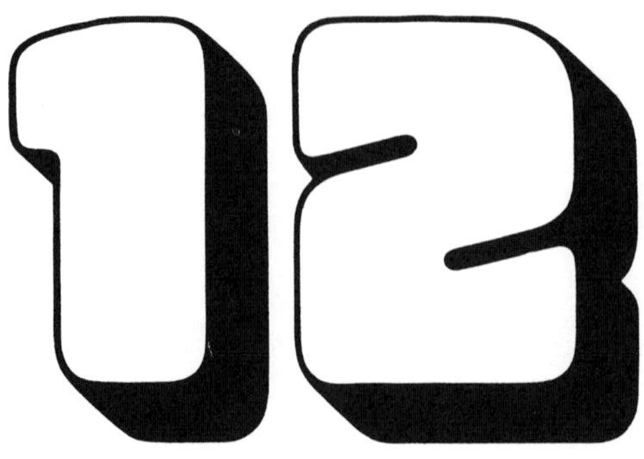

Musical variation = interfacing + data processing

Real musicians produce complex variations on musical themes, and in this way build words of music with a discernible structure, at least, discernible by the experts. Without being too ambitious, we can be confident of programming the computer to produce some fairly simple, possibly even crude, variations which are still quite interesting to listen to.

There are three such variations that we shall tackle. I have called them

reverse
invert
permute

The simplest of the three is *reverse*. All this does is to reverse the order of the notes in the tune, so that, when played, in effect, it is played backwards.

The next one, *invert*, turns tunes upside-down. Any sequence of notes that is rising in pitch is replaced by one that is falling in pitch. The way we shall do this is to consider each note in turn, calculate how many tones higher it is than the middle note of our keyboard, and replace it by a note which is the same number of tones lower than that. And, of course, vice versa. The tune you get by inverting another tune has a completely different character, and can be quite fascinating.

Lastly there is *permute*. This takes the notes of the tune in small groups of fixed length, and reverses the order of the notes in each group, while preserving the order of the groups themselves. For example, permuting the following sequence in groups of 4:

abcdefghijklmnop

would yield:

dcbahgfelkjiponm

Of course, all this is still a far cry from the beautiful effects of more sophisticated variations which a musically talented human being is capable of making. All the same, even for a musician, it could be quite useful to experiment with the kind of program we shall build, if only to try out ideas, saving an lot of time which would be spent if the donkey work were carried out by a human.

Although we have introduced these three variations as exercises in musical composition, in fact, when we turn to the programming, it can be seen that all we shall be doing is to carry out various curious transformations to strings of characters. And the interesting thing is that an enormous amount of computing that goes on in the real world of commerce, of science, and of industry, boils down to carrying out transformations of strings of characters. The same can be said of text-processing, which is used not only in commerce, science, and industry, but also by authors of books (for example this one).

Interfaces

In considering what has to be done by each subroutine, we shall of course assume that immediately before calling it, our main program will call *get tune,* and, immediately after it has done its task and produced a variation, the main program will call *store tune.* As a consequence of this, we know where to expect the raw data to be, (that is, where *get tune* puts it – in *a*$). Similarly, we need to decide where to put the result (where the main program will expect to find it).

Making subroutines fit together from the outside in this way is quite independent of what happens inside them. It is rather like having a set of boxes which you can fit together so that they lock, because the outsides have the right, matching, shapes.

This idea is so important in computing that it has a special, technical name which you are sure to come across. It is called *interfacing.* The kind of interfacing we have just been talking about is called *software interfacing,* because it is about interfacing between program modules. Programs are called software because they can be easily changed or modified. In contrast, the parts of the computer such as chips, circuits, electronic gadgetry and so on are called *hardware.*

Sometimes, before two separate pieces of computer hardware can be connected together and used, they have to be provided with extra pieces of hardware and software which make them fit together. These are called interfaces. For example, you need an interface in order to be able to connect a micro-drive to your computer. The interface unit made by Sinclair for this purpose contains other interfaces too. One of these is called an 'RS 232' interface, which is a well-defined standard for the computer industry, and is used by many pieces of equipment, such as Visual Display units (VDUs), printers, and communications devices.

When a piece of equipment, like a printer, is connected to a computer, in addition to them both needing to have matching hardware interfaces, the computer has to be provided with a program which sends the data to the printer at the speed required by it, and in chunks the right size (usually a line at a time). Line-length (the maximum number of characters in a line) can vary, and this has to be controlled by the interface program, which is said to *drive* the printer. The printer-driver program (or printer interface program) also has to deal with the control characters which are to be sent to the printer, causing it to provide operations like starting a new line, starting a new page, setting tabs, and so on. And that's not all. The program is getting the data for the printer from somewhere in the computer's memory. So it has to know where in memory, how much there is, and the exact format used for storing it. So you can see that interfacing plays a vital role in computing, even though it often goes on behind the scenes without your having to worry about it, or even realize how much work of this kind is being done.

Reversing the order of a string

The easiest way to produce a new string in reverse order is to use another string variable to store it. If the new string variable is called *e$*, then we can first give *e$* the value of the empty string, and then glue on to it each character of *a$* in turn; of course we start at the end of *a$* and work backwards:

```
LET e$ = ""
FOR z = LEN a$ TO 1 STEP -1
LET e$ = e$ + a$(z)
NEXT z
```

This works perfectly well.

However, it is a bit wasteful, both of the computer's memory, and of its time, because the computer has to spend a lot of time glueing together, and because you use up as much space again, in *e$*, as you are already using in *a$*.

An alternative, more efficient method is to swap appropriate pairs of characters in *a*$. The first pair to swap is first and last; the second pair to swap is second and one before last, and so on.

The loop to do this must go only halfway through the length of *a*$, because then every appropriate pair will have been swapped:

```
2030>LET len=LEN a$
2040 LET mid=INT (0.1+len/2)
2050 FOR z=1 TO mid
2060 LET k$=a$(z): LET a$(z)=a$(len-z+1): LET a$(1
en-z+1)=k$
2070 NEXT z
```

The value of *mid* is halfway through *a*$. Notice that it does not matter whether the length of *a*$ is an odd or an even number of characters. For example, if the length is 13, the value of *mid* will be 6. The swaps will be between:

1	and	13
2	and	12
3	and	11
4	and	10
5	and	9
6	and	8

The 7th character is the middle one, and is not swapped with anything. If the length is 12 instead of 13, the value of *mid* will still be 6, but the swaps will be between:

1	and	12
2	and	11
3	and	10
4	and	9
5	and	8
6	and	7

There is an even number of characters, so there is no middle one left over.

And you should check out for yourself that the expression (len − z + 1) always gives the subscript for the other member of the pair to be swapped, (for every value of *z* from 1 to *k*).

Inverting a string

Since what we want to turn upside-down are the pitch-values, we need to remind ourselves of the relation between the pitch of a note and the character that is stored for it in a TUNE string. Referring back to the subroutine that set up the keyboard, we used an array *k* to store the pitch-values, so that later we could use this array as a look-up table. The loop which set up the look-up table by storing pitch-values in the array, was:

```
670>FOR j=1TO LEN s$
680 LET pitch=bottom p +j-1
690 LET k(CODE s$(j))=pitch
700 NEXT j
```

To invert a TUNE, we look at each note in turn and find its pitch, say *oldpz*; and that part is easy, as you can see by looking at line 690. We use the look-up table, and get the pitch of the first note in *a*$, by writing:

LET p1 = k(CODE a$(1))

To get the pitch of each note in turn after that we shall of course use a loop. If *z* is the loop control variable, then inside the loop, we can write:

LET oldpz = k(CODE a$(z))

When the tune has been inverted, each note will have a pitch which is the same distance from the top note of the range as the old note was from the bottom. Thus the middle note of the range will not change, low notes become high, and high notes become low. The top and bottom notes of the range were fixed (line 660) in the subroutine which initialized the musical keyboard. Their values are held in the variables *top p,* and *bottom p*. If we call the new, inverted pitch *new pz,* then its value will be produced by

LET newpz = top p — (oldpz — bottom p)

Having found the new pitch for each note, we have to 'translate' this into its appropriate character representation on the keyboard. This is one of the characters in the string *s*$ that was used to do this coding in the first place, and the pitch value is nothing more than the position of the character in *s*$. If you need to remind yourself about this, look at lines 610 to 700 (listed in Chapter 9). You can see from line 640 that when the variable *j* is used for the position:

pitch = *bottom* + *j* — 1

However, we know the pitch, and want the position, *j*. So we can calculate it by writing

LET j = pitch — bottom + 1

Putting all this together, the main body of the *invert* subroutine will be as follows:

```
2130>FOR z=1TO LEN a$
2140 LET oldpz=k(CODE a$(z))
2150 LET newpz=top p-(oldpz-bottom p)
2160 LET position=newpz+1-bottom p
2170 LET a$(z)=s$(position)
2180 NEXT z
```

Although this is a short piece of program, it is doing some tricky arithmetic. When writing this it is much easier to work it out and get it right if you choose suitable names for the variables. For example, *oldpz* for the old pitch, and *newpz* for the new pitch of each note, and *position* for the position in the string *s*$ of the required character.

Permutations on a string

We have already seen how to reverse a string. Now we can apply the technique to reversing each short substring in a string.

It would be convenient if we could divide the whole string *a*$ exactly into a number of groups of equal length and have no characters left over. In other words, first of all, find a factor of the length of *a*$. If we limit ourselves to looking for the highest factor which is not greater than 7, we can write a loop which has the structural form:

LET z = 7 TO 2 STEP − 1

if z is a factor of LEN a$ then jump out of the loop

NEXT z

Of course, that is not BASIC, but it is a good way of expressing what we want to do. How can we test whether *z* is a factor of some integer, say *l*? There is a standard way of doing this, by testing the expression

$$l = z*\text{INT}(l/z)$$

If this equality expression is true, then *z* must be a factor of *l*. This is so because the function INT throws away any fractional part of the value of *l*/*z*, and keeps only the integer part. So multiplying by *z* again will only give *l* as a result if there was no fractional part in the answer to the division.

Just in case the length of *a*$ is not exactly divisible by *any* of the integers between 2 and 7, we can start by assigning the full length of *a*$ as the value of *factor*.

So the first part of our subroutine will be:

```
2240>LET len=LEN a$:LET factor=len
2250 FOR z=7 TO 2 STEP -1
2260 IF len=z*INT (len/z) THEN   LET factor=z: GO
TO 2280
2270 NEXT z
```

On arrival at line 2280, *factor* will have a value which exactly divides *len,* usually some value like 7 or less, but, in awkward cases, the value of *len* itself.

The number of *times* we want to reverse a group of characters of length *factor* is *len*/*factor.* So we can find that value by

LET times = len/factor

or, with more reliability,

LET times = INT(0.1 + len/factor)

Suppose we think about what we want to do each *time* we have such a group. This is going to be a few lines of program very similar to lines 2050 to 2070. Very similar, but not identical, because we want to do it many times using different groups of characters. Let's rewrite it in a more general way. If *first* is the position in *m*$ of the first character of a group, *mid* is the position of the middle character and *last* the position of the last character, all in the same group, we can write

```
2310>FOR y=firstTO mid
2320 LET k$=a$(y): LET a$(y)=a$(last-y+first): LET
 a$(last-y+first)=k$
2330 NEXT y
```

That is equivalent to the original, when *first* = 1, and *last* = *k*; and those are the right values for the first group. For the next group, we need to add the value of *factor*, both to *first* and to *last*. In fact we need to do that as many times as there are groups. That means another loop round the one just written, with a calculation for *k* and *times* before it. The complete subroutine becomes:

```
2240>LET len=LEN a$:LET factor=len
2250 FOR z=7 TO 2 STEP -1
2260 IF len=z*INT (len/z) THEN   LET factor=z: GO
TO 2280
2270 NEXT z
```

```
2280 REM factor divides len exactly
2290 LET first=1: LET last=factor: LET mid=INT (0.
1+factor/2): LET times=INT (0.1+len/factor)
2300 FOR z=1 TO times
2310 FOR y=first TO mid
2320 LET k$=a$(y): LET a$(y)=a$(last-y+first): LET
 a$(last-y+first)=k$
2330 NEXT y
```

13

Mix and match

Simple matching of tune and rhythm

The aim of the MUSIC PROGRAM is to have the computer produce pieces of music, not just sequences of notes of equal length, nor sequences representing rhythms which sound vaguely like morse code. Now, in order to produce any particular piece of music, we have to combine the information contained in two strings, the TUNE string, and the RHYTHM string. Each note we give the computer to play, uses the BEEP instruction, and this requires two pieces of data to go with it, first the duration of the note and secondly the pitch. The duration is obtained from the rhythm string, and the pitch from the tune string. But in both cases, a little unravelling is needed to provide a suitable interface between the way the data is represented and stored in the strings, and the way we have to represent it in the BEEP instruction. The stored strings use tokens; the BEEP instruction uses numbers.

We have already seen how to unravel the pitch information when we looked at how to invert a tune. It was a matter of using the look-up table of data stored in the *k*( ) array, (keyboard array), together with the *s*$ string which stores the order of the keytop symbols just the way they are laid out on the keyboard.

Given the keytop token, its CODE tells us its position in the *k*( ) array, and the value stored at that position in the array is the pitch. Thus if the token is stored in, say, *c*$, then *pitch* can be obtained by writing:

```
LET pitch = k(CODE(c$))
```

To unravel the duration data from the rhythm string, we again have to translate the *character* representation of the tokens into numbers. Now the CODEs for the digits Ø to 9 are in the same order as the digits, and increase by 1 for each digit, while the CODE for ':' (colon), which we use to represent 1Ø, is 1 more than the CODE for 9. So all that is required to translate a character is to subtract the CODE for 'Ø' from the character CODE. If the character CODE is stored in *c*$, then to obtain *duration,* we can write:

```
LET duration = CODE(c$) – CODE("Ø")
```

Now a rhythm string and a tune string for the same musical melody will always, of course, have the same length, since each is storing data for the same number of notes (one the duration and the other the pitch of each note). So if we use the *get rhythm* subroutine, which copies the RHYTHM string into *a*$, we can copy this into, say, *d*$, and then use the *get tune* subroutine, which will copy the TUNE string into *a*$, we could use the following program to play the melody:

```
FOR z = LEN a$
LET duration = CODE d$(z) – CODE("Ø")
LET pitch – k(CODE(a$(z)))
BEEP duration*Ø.1, pitch
NEXT z
```

The duration has been multiplied by Ø.1, because the stored duration was in arbitrary units, the shortest note being of length 1, and this would mean 1 second to BEEP. One second is a very long duration for a short note, so we divide it by 1Ø.

That's fine for matching up a tune and a rhythm of equal length. But we would like to do more interesting things, like playing the tune of one melody to the rhythm of a strange melody, and these will probably have different lengths.

Mixed Marriages

Suppose we wanted to marry a TUNE of length 12 notes to a RHYTHM of length 7 notes. One way of doing it is to repeat the TUNE 7 times and repeat the RHYTHM 12 times. Then we have a TUNE and a RHYTHM of equal length – 84 notes. If the RHYTHM was 28 notes instead of 7, we could still use 84, because 84 is exactly divisible by 28, as well as by 12 and by 7.

In fact for any two lengths, the new length we would find convenient to use is the number which is the *least common multiple* of the original two lengths. That is, the smallest number which is exactly divisible by both the lengths. One way of finding this is first to find their *highest common factor,* and to multiply that by the remaining factors. For example, if 12 and 28 are the two lengths, and writing HCF for the highest common factor, and LCM for least common multiple.

$12 = 2 \times 2 \times 3$
$28 = 2 \times 2 \times 7$

So HCF = 4
$12 \div 4 = 3$
$28 \div 4 = 7$
So LCM $= 4 \times 3 \times 7 = 84$

84 is the smallest number which is exactly divisible by both 12 and 28.

Finding a simple way to go about finding the HCF of two numbers on a computer is not all that obvious, but fortunately, a talented Greek called Euclid discovered a way of doing it more than 2000 years ago. The computers in those days were less sophisticated and quite a bit slower than nowadays, so it is a tribute to his ingenuity that his method is still highly suitable.

Euclid's invention for finding HCF

It is much easier to learn how to do it than to understand why it works, but it always does, and here's what you do. First, we'll do it with no computer, just pencil and paper:

Step 1 Write down the two numbers, the larger one on the left.

Step 2 Divide the larger by the smaller, and throw away the answer, *but keep a note of the remainder.*

Step 3 Write down two new numbers, the first (on the left) being the one previously written on the right (in step 1), and the second (on the right) being the remainder you kept a note of.

Step 4 If the number on the right is Ø, then the number on the left is the HCF!
If it isn't, go back to *Step 2* and continue.

Doing this with 28 and 12, we get:

28	12	(28 ÷ 12 = 2, and remainder 4)
12	4	(12 ÷ 4 = 3, and remainder Ø)
4	Ø	

This method always struck me as extremely clever, and also reminded me of the story I was taught at school as a child, about what happened in history when some intrepid adventurer first brought some strange and exotic leaves to England from somewhere in the East. He said it was called 'tea', and that what you did was to pour boiling water on to the leaves for a few minutes. Some people did this, then strained off the water and tasted the tea-leaves. My own theory is that this is why tea didn't catch on in most countries.

But of course, those people who were as bright as Euclid, or who remembered his invention, were clever enough to throw away the tea-leaves and drink the water. And that is why *step 2* of Euclid's method always reminds me of this story.

The only tricky thing to program for a computer in all this is finding the remainder when you divide say, x by y. It is all made easy by using the INT function, which keeps the whole number (the integer) part of a number and throws away the fraction. (When you come to think about it, the secret of success all through life is knowing what to keep, and what to throw away).

Breaking it into simple steps

(1) Divide x by y.
(2) Take the INT part. (Throw away the fraction.)
(3) Multiply by y.
(4) Subtract the answer from x.

What you have left is the remainder. And this can all be said in one line, using BASIC

LET remainder = x − y*INT(x/y)

So, to find the HCF of the lengths of *a*$ and *d*$:

```
4060>LET alen=LEN a$:LET dlen=LEN d$
4070 IF alen>dlen THEN  LET big=alen: LET small=dl
en: GO TO 4090
4080 LET big=dlen: LET small=alen
4090 LET rem=big-small*INT (big/small)
4100 IF rem=0 THEN  GO TO 4130
4110 LET big=small: LET small=rem
4120 GO TO 4090
4130 LET hcf=small
```

The lines 4070 and 4080 were concerned only with making sure that the bigger of the two lengths was stored in *big*, and the smaller was stored in *small*. But the interesting piece of program is 4090 to 4130.

It has a structure which is worth looking at, and it is worth drawing a program pattern box for it. The structure is a very general one. It can be used for *any loop you want to program.* In the diagram, I use a box to indicate the body of the loop, that is, the lines that get repeated.

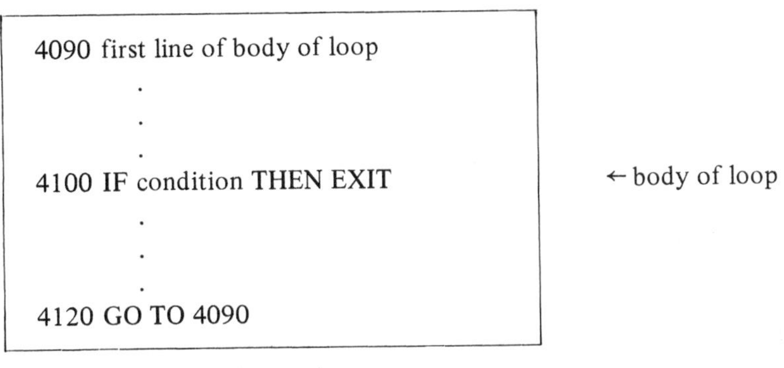

Program pattern box for a loop

The EXIT line, 4100, can be anywhere inside such a loop and it always has the form

IF condition THEN GO TO n

where *n* is the first line following the loop, In theprogram for HCF, the exit line happens to come second in the body of the loop. In some loops, it is the first line, in others it is the last line. Where it occurs is a matter of convenience. But basically, there has to be an exit line which is a conditional instruction – that means it begins with IF and ends with a GO TO that takes the computer out of the loop. The end of the body of the loop is a simple GO TO back to the beginning.

One of the effects of using a program pattern with a well-defined structure like this is that it makes it easier for you to get your program right. For example, using this structure, when the computer gets to line 3960, we *know* we can rely on the fact that the last remainder was zero. So we can be sure that the sum has been properly finished as we intended when we wrote the program.

Having found the HCF, we can find the LCM by dividing both lengths by the HCF to find the factors which are not common to them both. Multiplying these together with the HCF gives the LCM:

```
4140>LET a factor=dlen/hcf
4150 LET d factor=alen/hcf
4160 LET lcm=a factor*d factor*hcf
```

You can see that *afactor* is the number of times we shall have to repeat *a*$, and *dfactor* is the number of times we shall have to repeat *d*$, in order to make two new strings the same length, out of the TUNE and the RHYTHM strings.

We shall store the new strings in two new arrays, *u*\$( ) for the TUNE, and *v*\$( ) for the RHYTHM. The piece of program for making each new string is very similar. Let's start with the TUNE string, which is stored in *a*\$. Its length is *alen,* and we have to store it in *u*\$ *afactor* times. The first time we store it, we could write:

LET s\$(1 TO alen) = a\$

the second time

LET u\$(1 + alen TO alen + alen) = a\$

and we have to do that, *afactor* times, so we can use a FOR loop:

```
4190>DIM u$(lcm)
4200 LET first=1: LET last=alen
4210 FOR z=1 TO a factor
4220 LET u$(first TO last)=a$
4230 LET first=first+alen
4240 LET last=last+alen
4250 NEXT z
```

Similarly, for the *d*\$ string; but this one has to be repeated *dfactor* times, and the length added to *first* and *last* each time is of course *dlen*:

```
4260>DIM v$(lcm)
4270 LET first=1: LET last=dlen
4280 FOR z=1 TO d factor
4290 LET v$(first TO last)=d$
4300 LET first=first+dlen
4310 LET last=last+dlen
4320 NEXT z
```

We now have the data organized into a suitable structure for playing our musical composition but, as usual, the actual form of each piece of data is of the wrong type to give to BEEP, because it is a token, not a number. But the translation from character type to number type is exactly as we did it for two strings of equal length earlier in this chapter. The only difference is that the data is in two arrays instead of two simple strings. But the program needed is almost identical:

```
4360>FOR z=1TO lcm
4370 LET duration=CODE v$(z)-CODE "0"
4380 LET pitch=k(CODE u$(z))
4390 BEEP duration*0.1,pitch
4400 NEXT z
```

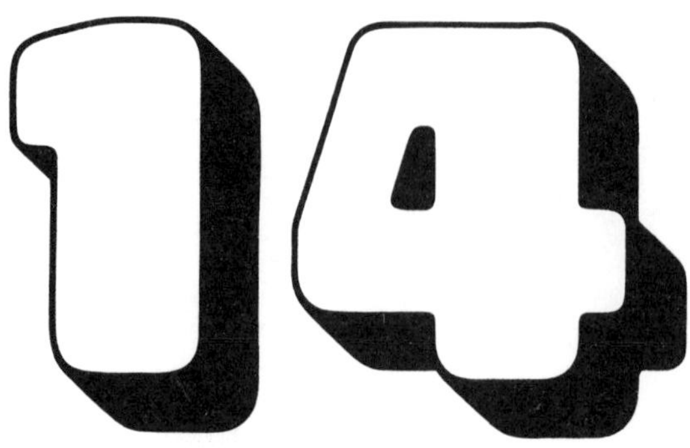

14 Menus and look-up tables

We have covered quite a lot of ground writing small programs (using 'programs' in a very general sense – for almost all of them have been written as subroutines). 'Small' is of course relative, but it is useful to endow it with a special, technical sense in relation to programs and programming, because the problems of writing a small program are different from those of writing a large one. The difference is not merely one of scale.

The essential feature of a 'small' program is that its small size enables the human mind to 'take it in' as a whole, without getting lost in its detailed structure. For this to be so, it is vital that it all go on one page when written or printed out. From this point of view, one full screen is very small, because it will not always accommodate even a 'small' program. If you have to scroll more than once to see all the program, you can't see it as a whole in your mind, quite apart from on the screen. In contrast to small programs, a large program can be seen as a whole only if it is presented in a summary form which shows its structure, without getting you lost in the intricacies of its detail, which spreads into many pages.

Menu programs

Many of the subroutines we have developed up to this point were concerned with using the computer to compose and play tunes and variations of tunes. They were written with the idea always in the background that they could be brought together in a large program; and with this end in mind, some attention was paid to their having compatible interfaces. Here is a list of them, in small groups whose members are obviously logically connected:

set up musical keyboard
play musical keyboard
strum

reverse
invert
permute

combine tune and rhythm
lcm
marry
play opus

store tune
get tune
replay tune
alter tune

store rhythm
get rhythm
replay rhythm
alter rhythm

Now, although this is a useful group of subroutines, you can see that figuring out how to tie them together into one program is a new kind of problem that we haven't yet been faced with. Looking at the list, you could at a stretch think of it as a kind of menu, but not a very helpful kind of menu, because you can't really tell even what to choose, let alone how to combine things. It is almost as bad an imitation of a real menu as if you went into a restaurant and were presented with a list that read:

slicing
peeling
dicing
quartering

veal
beef
lamb
chicken
fish

tomatoes
peas
potatoes
mushrooms
beans

french dressing
mustard
tartare sauce
mint jelly

salad
cucumber
beetroot

frying
boiling
grilling
roasting
stewing
casserole

rye bread
wholemeal bread
french bread

This is less a menu than a list of ingredients and methods for constructing one. But before you can construct one, you need to know how you want your food prepared and cooked, and which dishes should go together. A similar difficulty confronts someone utterly unfamiliar with Chinese food, on entering a Chinese restaurant and reading the list of separate dishes you can have. (For this reason, many Chinese restaurants append suggested complete balanced meal menus in addition to the complete list of dishes, on the menu card for their diners.)

Most computer games, and many business packages now incorporate menu presentation of their facilities. This means that the user needs little or no training in using the package, provided he or she understands what it is for, and what he or she wants to do with it. A menu provides a structural skeleton for what the user wants to do, as well as providing choices at one, two or more levels. This is analogous to another kind of restaurant menu, one which gives a set meal consisting of a fixed number of courses. For each course, you may make a choice. Sometimes this is a simple choice of one item from a list, sometimes it is one item from one list (say main meat or fish dish) plus any two items from another list (say vegetables).

There are two aspects of menus which are of interest in program construction. One is that they help you to think about the program in structural terms. The other aspect is how to implement a menu itself as a subroutine which forms part of the program. First we shall look at the structural aspect.

Structure

The idea behind the MUSIC PROGRAM is not quite like a set meal, because there is no special course you start with or finish with. There are a number of 'courses', but you can start with any one you like, go to another, come back again, and generally pick and choose what to do next, until *you* decide to stop.

Of course, there is no simple, inescapable, or only correct way of structuring this or any other program, but in planning a structure, it will be useful only if the structure is a suitable skeleton for the body and body-functions and clothes that we want to flesh it out with and dress it up in. Looking again at the list of subroutines we have, we can visualize a menu whose main headings (or courses) are:

TUNES
VARIATIONS (on tunes)
RHYTHMS
COMPOSITIONS (combining tunes and rhythms)

and to illustrate the structure of this, we can use a diagram which is similar to a family tree.

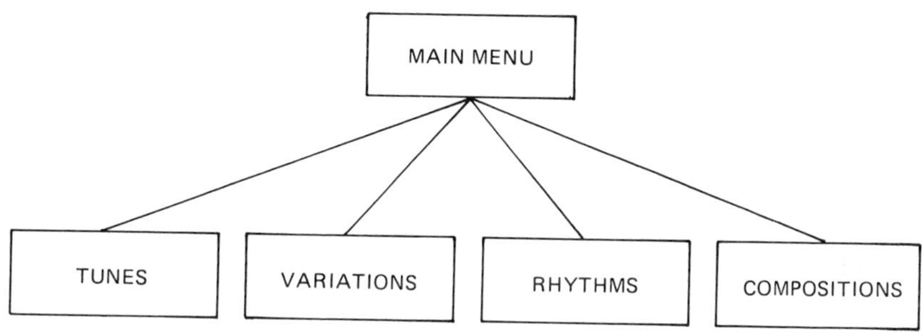

Each of the four boxes that can be chosen from the main menu can itself be regarded as a sub-menu, and, again bearing our list of existing subroutines in mind, we can produce the following four sub-menus:

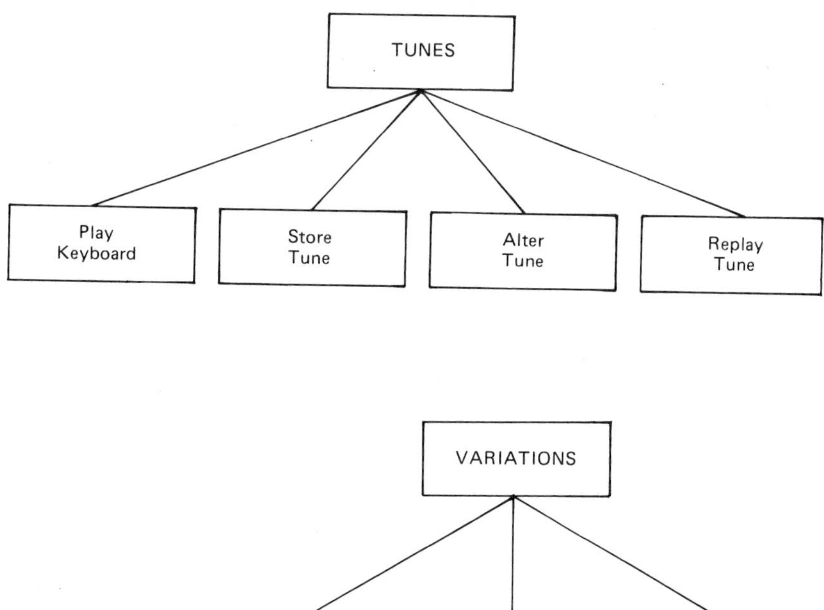

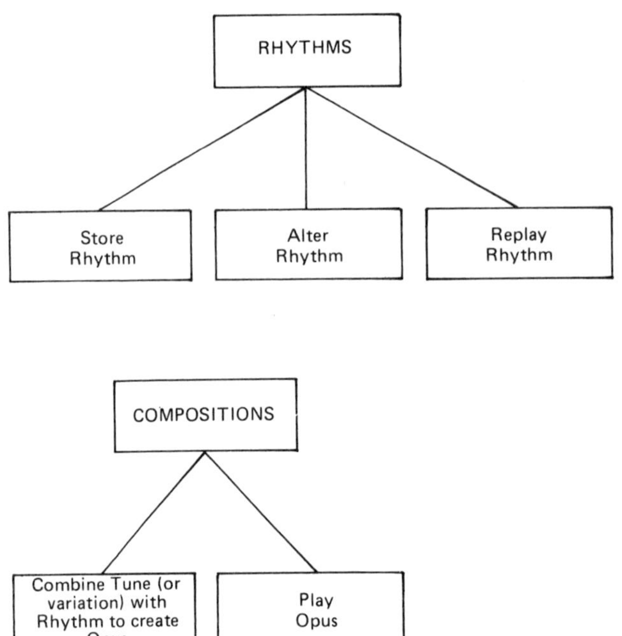

Each of these four sub-menus can be regarded as being at the same level as each other, but all one level lower than the main menu. This becomes more obvious if we combine the five menus into one structure diagram.

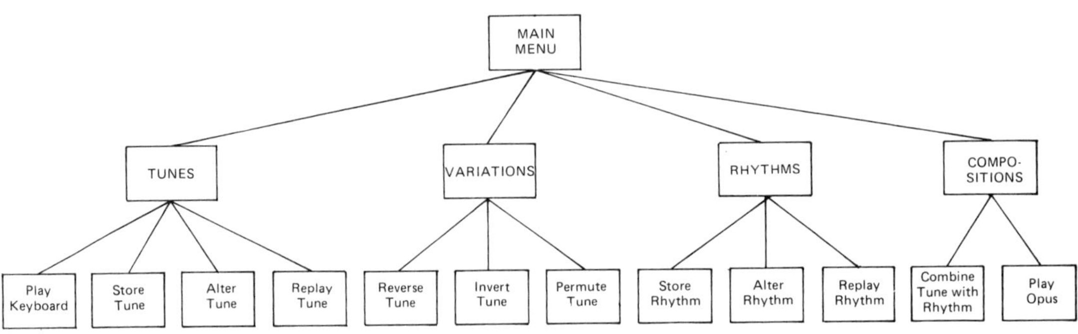

This diagram begins to suggest the structure of the program, to suggest how our various subroutines should be linked together. It is certainly not complete, but it can be developed and refined later. Right now, let us turn our attention to the main menu. What should it do? What should it look like? How do we make a program that implements it?

What it should do is present to the user a number of choices, ask the user to indicate the preferred choice by input of a prescribed and simple kind, test the input to find which choice has been made, and then GOSUB to the appropriate subroutine (in this instance a sub-menu). At the moment, we have listed just four choices, but most menus should have three standard choices in addition to the particular ones. The first of these should enable the user to exit, that is return to the previous higher level. This of course, doesn't apply to the main menu, which has no higher level. It will apply to the sub-menus, which have the main menu as a higher level to which the user may wish to RETURN, in order to select a different sub-menu. The second standard choice should provide the user with helpful information about how to use the program, what it does, etc. A feature of this kind is now common in many computing systems, and is usually called HELP. (This is so widespread that whenever you are using any system which you are not familiar with, it is quite a good idea to type in HELP, and see what happens). The third choice is one which allows the user to say, in effect, 'I have had enough of this program, at least for the time being, and want to STOP'. So we shall include these three choices in our menus (but leave out RETURN in the main menu). What the menu *actually* looks like leaves plenty of scope for artistic layout, eye-catching colour, and snazzy use of flashing messages. But these are more detail of presentation – important of course, but they don't affect the general idea that we are discussing at the moment. Here is an example of what the main menu looks like on the screen, using a simple presentation:

```
                    music program
                      MAIN MENU

Sub-menus available                          token
---------------------------------------------------
    HELP (i.e. info)                           h
    TUNES                                      t
    VARIATIONS                                 v
    RHYTHMS                                    r
    COMPOSE                                    c
    STOP                                     STOP

CHOOSE SUB-MENU

enter token          "?"
```

The bottom line of the screen would show, not a question mark, as printed above, but a flashing cursor. When the user enters a selected token, it is displayed in the position marked by the cursor.

Now we have sorted our ideas about this menu, we can start to think about the program to implement it. What does it have to do? Its tasks are:

(1) Print the screen display (as shown above).
(2) Check the user has input a valid token, and, if not, tell him so and give him another chance.
(3) Transfer control to the appropriate subroutine, using the address which corresponds to the choice the user makes – one out of six possibilities.

Let us deal with the first two tasks, and then review the situation.

The instructions necessary to display the menu involve a fair amount of detailed specification to get the layout right; and the TAB instruction, which can be included among the items list in a PRINT instruction, is very useful:

TAB 29

tells the printer to move to column 29 of the display before printing the next character. Before looking at the program given below, you should try this for yourself. The easy way is to make a rough guess at the number of spaces, and TAB positions required; then run the few lines of program, and after you have seen what is produced, it is easy to edit it until it is right. The important things to remember in designing a menu layout are that it must be easy to read and understand; it must all fit into one screen; and if extra lines get printed in the lower (input) section of the screen, don't forget that the computer scrolls the screen up a line or two to make room, so always start your menu with a few blank lines at the beginning of the first PRINT instruction.

```
1620>CLS :PRINT '''TAB 9;"music program"';TAB 11;"
MAIN MENU"''
1630 PRINT "Sub-menus available          token"'"....
...............                   ....."''
1640 PRINT "   HELP (ie info)";TAB 29;"h"''
1650 PRINT "   TUNES";TAB 29;"t"''
1660 PRINT "   VARIATIONS";TAB 29;"v"''
1670 PRINT "   RHYTHMS";TAB 29;"r"''
1680 PRINT "   COMPOSE";TAB 29;"c"''
1690 PRINT "    STOP ";TAB 28;" STOP  "
1700 INPUT "CHOOSE SUB-MENU."'"Enter token",c$
```

Next we come to checking whether the token input by the user is a valid one. There is a simple way of doing this (which turns out to be very convenient when we come on to the third task as well). If all the valid tokens are used to make up a string, a simple loop can be used to check whether the input token matches each of the string tokens in turn. In the case of this menu, let us first assign the string of valid tokens to *x*\$:

1610 LET x\$ = "htvrc STOP "

Notice that the last token in the string is not the letter P, nor a space, but the token 'STOP'.

The INPUT instruction (line 1700) used the variable *c*\$ for the token input, so the loop required must check whether *c*\$ matches *x*\$(1), *x*\$(2), and so on, until a match is found. If it is, then there should be a jump out of the loop. That way, if the loop terminates without a jump, it means there was no match, so the token input was not a valid one. In the case of a valid token being found, it will be convenient if we know which position in the *x*\$ string gave the matching token – then we have a number to use, instead of a letter. Here is the loop:

```
1720>FOR z=1TO LEN x$
1730 LET choice=z
1740 IF c$=x$(z) THEN  GO TO 1770
1750 NEXT z
1760 INPUT "You entered """;CHR$ (CODE c$);"""",''
which is not in the menu."'"Try again",c$:      GO
TO  1700
```

A few words are necessary to explain one of the items in the INPUT list of line 1760. The item is

CHR$ (CODE *c*$)

It is there because we want the actual value of *c*$ printed at that point. If it were an item in a PRINT list instead of an INPUT list, we could just write *c*$. But if we wrote *c*$ in an INPUT list, the computer will treat it as a variable name, and expect the user to input a value to it. Any item we want printed in an INPUT list must be an expression whose value is a string, but we can't use the *name* of a variable, even though that is an expression whose value is a string.

The way out of this dilemma is to force the computer to *use* *c*$ as a value not a name. Writing CODE *c*$ makes the computer find the code value for the character stored in *c*$. Writing CHR$ in front of that makes the computer find the character whose code that is. So we go in a little circle to get back to the value of *c*$, which is what we want. If you find that difficult to follow, try entering the following sequence of direct commands to the computer:

```
LET c$ = "a"
PRINT CODE ("a")
PRINT CODE (c$)
PRINT CHR$(CODE("a"))
PRINT CHR$ (CODE(c$))
```

At this stage, it would be wise to test the menu program, before doing any more detailed writing. It is always possible to test incomplete fragments of programs, by using a dummy statement or two to make it appear complete. In this case, a suitable dummy statement is:

```
1770 PRINT "option chosen was number  "; choice: STOP
```

You can now enter

```
RUN 1610
```

as a direct command, and test the whole program including the menu as far as it goes at the present.

This method of developing you programs should be a general rule to follow. If you wait until you have even a whole page (still a small program!) of instructions before you test it, you are merely making life more difficult for yourself. It is very rare for even a small program to work faultlessly at first attempt. This is just as true for experienced and skilful professional programmers as it is for novices. By testing very small pieces of program at a time, you will find it much easier to find the errors and put them right. A mistake commonly made when *testing* a program, even a small fragment, is failure to test all the things the program is supposed to do. For example, in this case, be sure to test for both valid and invalid tokens input.

The third implementation task was to transfer control to the appropriate subroutine. This is where we take out the 'dummy' statement inserted for testing purposes, and replace it with 'real' program.

Look-up Tables

When the computer arrives at the 'dummy' statement, the variable *choice* has a value which gives the position in the *x*$ string of the input token. The *x*$ string is 6 tokens long, so the value of *choice* must be an integer in the range 1 to 6.

We have seen arrays used as look-up tables already, notably in Chapter 8. The basic idea is that you have an index number to the information you really want; and this index number is used as the subscript of the array element where the information is stored. Here we have 6 possible index-values. We should like to use each of them to index the line-number of a different subroutine which corresponds to the indexed choice. So we use an array, say *c*( ), to store the line-numbers of the appropriate subroutines. These subroutines have not even been written yet, but, in order to be able to test our look-up piece of program, we can provide dummies which are later expanded. Here is an example of a dummy subroutine for the TUNES sub-menu. It can later be expanded into the real thing:

```
1800 REM Tunes Sub-Menu subroutine
1810 PRINT "TUNES SUB-MENU NOT YET AVAILABLE"
1820 RETURN
```

On return to the main menu, whether from this dummy or from the real thing later, we need to put the user again in the position of selecting from the items of the main menu. So we must add an instruction to the main menu subroutine immediately following the GOSUB, to take control back to the beginning of the main menu:

```
1780 GO TO 1610
```

Notice that line 1610 is the one which assigns the string of valid tokesn to *x*$. It is important to put this right at the beginning of the subroutine, because every other menu will use its own, different string and may as well use *x*$ to store it in each case.

Having done this, we can enter the direct command

```
GOSUB 1610
```

and test the main menu together with calling the sub-menu. Try doing this, and you will see that something unforeseen happens. Unless you keep your eye glued to the screen, you won't see what happens at all, it is too fast. As soon as you enter a valid token, the print line from 1810 flashes on to the screen and off again too quickly for you to read it. This is because the first print line in the main menu includes a CLS. Although this situation is happening with only a dummy subroutine, it often crops up with real ones too, and one way to deal with it is to insert an INPUT instruction in order to hold things up and give the user time to read the screen. The program can't continue until the user inputs something – we don't actually care what is input. We'll rewrite the dummy subroutine as follows:

```
1800 REM Tunes Sub-Menu subroutine
1810 PRINT "TUNES SUB-MENU NOT YET AVAILABLE"
1820 INPUT "Enter any key to continue", c$
1830 RETURN
```

Now, at line 1820, the computer sits and waits for input, giving the user time to read the message at leisure, before hitting ENTER.

Once we have made sure our dummy subroutine call works, we can go ahead and set up a dummy subroutine for each of the other options. They will all be almost identical to the one above, but of course must use different line-numbers, and the print message will differ in just one word. Instead of TUNES, we shall need each of the other option names.

Let us suppose that we use the following line numbers for the start of these subroutines:

help	4610
tunes	1800
variations	4420
rhythms	3530
compose	3720
stop	590

Then we must ensure that at the beginning of our main program these numbers are stored in our look-up table, the array *c*( ). We can do this by using a DATA statement and a loop which READs its data values into the array *c*( ):

```
2730 RESTORE 2740
2740 DATA 4610, 1800, 4420, 3530, 3720, 590
2750 FOR z = 1 TO 6: READ c(z): NEXT z
```

We shall use a similar group of instructions to extend this subroutine line-number look-up table for each of the other menus; and it is convenient to use the same array, using an 'offset' value to indicate the beginning of each table. For example, there are 6 items in the first table. So the offset for the next table is 6, and the program to set it up might be

```
2760 LET table 2 offset = 6
2770 RESTORE 2780
2780 DATA 4610, 790, 990, 1290, 1390, 590
2790 LET table 3 offset = table 2 offset + 6
2800 FOR z = table 2 offset + 1 TO table 3 offset
2810 READ c(z)
2820 NEXT z
```

Each table gets a new offset value which is obtained by adding the length of the previous table to that table's offset value. You can picture the way the array is being used to produce the complete set of look-up tables:

Array *c*( )

Subscripts	**Contents**	
1	4610	↑
2	1800	
3	4420	**table 1**
4	3530	
5	3720	
6	590	↓
7	4610	↑
8	790	
9	990	**table 2** (offset value = length of table 1)
10	1290	
11	1390	
12	590	↓
13		↑
14		
		table 3 (offset value = table 2 offset + length of table 2)

The array *c*( ) will be used for each look-up table of subroutine line-numbers, each section corresponding to one menu.

To see how the pieces of menu implementation fit together, here is a complete subroutine, not for the main menu, but for the TUNES sub-menu.

```
1800>REM ************ Tunes Menu SUBr     *********
1810 LET x$="hpsra STOP "
1820 CLS : PRINT '''TAB 9;"music program"';TAB 8;"
TUNES  SUB-MENU"''
1830 PRINT "  choices available         token"'"  .
................          ....."
1840 PRINT "  HELP (ie info)";TAB 29;"h"''
1850 PRINT "  PLAY KEYBOARD";TAB 29;"p"''
1860 PRINT "  STORE TUNE";TAB 29;"s"''
1870 PRINT "  REPLAY TUNE";TAB 29;"r"''
1880 PRINT "  ALTER TUNE";TAB 29;"a"''
1890 PRINT "  EXIT (return to Main Menu)";TAB 29;"
e"''
1900 PRINT "   STOP ";TAB 28;" STOP "
1910 INPUT "CHOOSE OPTION."'"Enter token",c$
1920 FOR z=1 TO LEN x$
1930 LET choice=z
1940 IF c$=x$(z) THEN  GO TO 1980
1950 NEXT z
1960 IF c$="e" THEN  RETURN
1970 INPUT "You entered """;CHR$ (CODE c$);"""","'"
which is not in the menu."'"Try again",c$: GO TO 1
920
1980 GO SUB c(choice+t offset)
1990 GO TO 1810:                    REM *************
****** end of Tunes Menu SUBr ********************
```

There are two features which didn't arise in the main menu subroutine. One of these can be seen in line 1980. It follows from the discussion about table offsets. Instead of GOSUB *c*(*choice*) we have GOSUB *c*(*choice* + *t offset*) where *t offset* is the tunes table offset.

The other feature is the inclusion of the EXIT (return to main program) choice. This, by its very nature, cannot be treated as a GOSUB, because it is a RETURN (to where the tunes menu subroutine was itself called). So the way exit is dealt with is to test for it specially, whenever the user's input token fails to match with any of the valid tokens in the *x*$ string, before telling the user he got it wrong. So the test is inserted (line 1960) between the end of the token-matching loop and the 'try again' message.

That just about wraps up how to implement menus. All the other menus in the MUSIC PROGRAM are virtually the same.

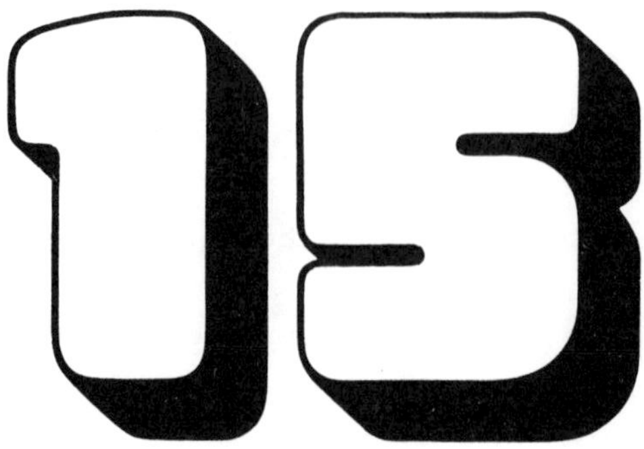

Program structure

Structuring your program

The MUSIC PROGRAM contains more than 550 BASIC lines, and a number of these are multiple-statement line. It takes about 32 screenfuls of listing. It is not a mammoth program but it is certainly large enough to illustrate that you can't write a program of any size without planning its structure in advance. You may be able to write some of the subroutines that provide the fundamental facilities, but it is a hopeless task to try to string them together without an overall plan which shows how the program as a whole is made up of its constituent parts, and their relation to one another. That is what is meant by program structure.

We talked about program structure just a little when discussiong menus in Chapter 14. But there we restricted our view to the structure of the main menu. It is fairly clear that there is more to this program than the menus. Before the user can be presented with the main menu, the program must set up the musical keyboard, set up the look-up tables containing the subroutine line-numbers (used in all the menus), assign initial values to a whole number of variables, and provide DIM statements for all the arrays to be used.

One picture is worth a thousand words, and this is certainly true when describing the structure of a program. So far, we have said that our program is made up as follows:

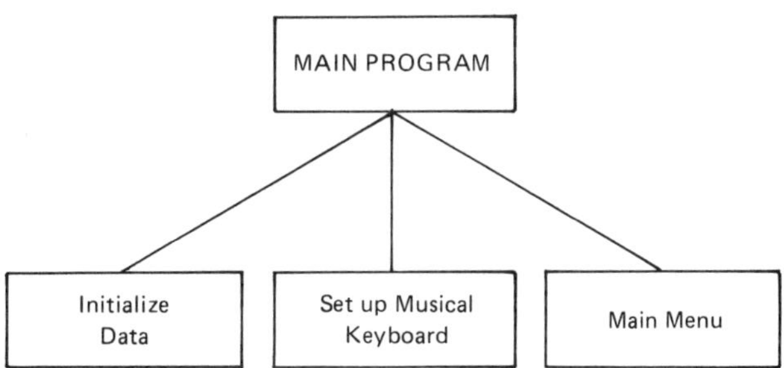

Each of these three main parts of the program can of course itself be broken down to show its constituent parts. We have already done this in the case of Main Menu. Setting up the Musical Keyboard is a much smaller program – we tackled it at the beginning of Chapter 8, and it took only twenty lines of BASIC. Initializing variables and arrays needs careful thought and more analysis of its structure is called for. This part of the program is concerned with setting up and organizing the data which the rest of the program will use. This data itself has structure. We have already been looking at the structure of the look-up tables used in the program. So far, 'Initialize Data' itself seems to have 3 parts.

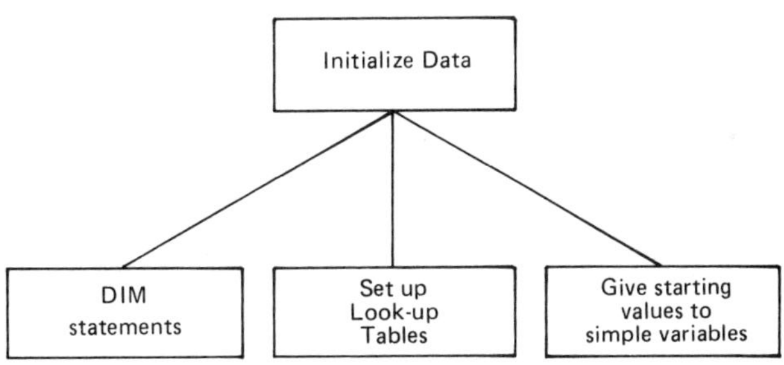

In order to survey the data that is used, it is worth setting out a list of the important variables and arrays that will be used by the various parts of the program

m$	string for storing tunes
l( )	array for lengths of tunes
n$( )	array for names of tunes
no of tunes	
r$	string for storing rhythms
s( )	array for sizes of rhythms
i( )	array for identifiers of rhythms
no of rhythms	
max	maximum no of tunes and maximum no of rhythms
c( )	array used as look-up table for all menu choices the offsets in the *c*( ) array, which indicates the start of choices:
t offset	tunes-menu choices,
r offset	rhythms-menu choices,
c offset	compose-menu choices,
v offset	variations-menu choices

With any program that is not trivially small, there are many times when you want to change a decision you made about how to deal with some part of the program, either while it is still being developed, or after it is 'finished'. Programs are always being revised, improved, modified. So it is important to write it in such a way that it is easy to modify. For example, there are four arrays which have the same size. Their DIM statements all use the variable *max*. If it is decided to change the value of *max*, then only one program change is needed, not four.

Another example of this is the Choice look-up table offset values. If an extra choice is put into one of the menus, this will change *all* the offsets which follow. But *only one change* is required in the program provided each offset value is expressed, not as a simple number, but as the sum of the length and offset for the previous table.

One of the commonest causes of program crashes is that the programmer forgot to initialize one or another of the variables. A pair you might easily forget in this program are *m*$ and *r*$. The point to be made is the same for each so I will only talk about *m*$. This is the string variable which is used for storing all the TUNE strings. Each time a new TUNE string is to be stored, it is done by obeying the instruction

```
1070 LET m$ = m$ + a$
```

When the very first TUNE is to be stored, *m*$ will have nothing in it, but, unless *m*$ already exists as a program variable, the computer will crash the program at this line, because *m*$ is an unknown variable. So it has to be initialized by assigning to it the empty string

```
LET m$ = ""
```

Rhythm and tune data

One of the modifications I made to the MUSIC PROGRAM after I had written it and was trying it out was to provide some ready-made tunes and rhythms, because this made it much easier to use all the facilities of the program right away.

As a result, the structure of INITIALIZE DATA was changed in order to include a new section – a subroutine which set up the data for several tunes and rhythms, and which was called by the general initialize subroutine.

Each of the tunes and rhythms needed to be stored in *m$* and *r$*, but it was necessary to by-pass that part of the store-tune subroutine (and of the store-rhythm subroutine) which asks the user to input the token-string and its name. This was done by using GOSUBs to those subroutines, using line-numbers for an appropriate later entry point in them, after the token-string and name had already been entered. In other words, a slightly modified interface to them was used.

Seeing the program as a whole

For a large program, it is usually difficult to get a *complete* structure diagram on to one sheet of paper, but it is very useful to construct one that is as complete as is practicable on a single sheet of paper, because there is no other way you can 'see' the program in its entirety. Any of the boxes which there is no room to expand on that sheet can be expanded separately on other sheets.

Another thing is that the data structures are as important as the program structure, and it is very helpful to your programming if there is a clear indication on your structure diagram of the main data structures, and which parts of the program access them. This has been done in the diagram for the MUSIC PROGRAM (see next page).

The number shown in each box is the line number of the subroutine that does what is written in the box. Filling in these line-numbers as you are writing the program serves a double purpose. First of all, it helps you find things in your program. Secondly, where there is no line-number, it is an indication that this piece of program is still to be written. (The second line number, followed by an "R", refers to the renumbered version of the complete program in APPENDIX 3.)

Modifying a program with the help of a structure diagram

Programs constantly need modifying. If they are well structured, and you know what the structure is, the work of modification is much easier. Using the MUSIC program as described so far, led to the conclusion that a worthwhile improvement would be achieved if

(i) the range of note-durations was increased from (1–10) to (1–16);
(ii) pauses or rests of stated durations could be introduced into the compositions.

To fit the representation of a pause into the existing scheme is not difficult, and a fairly obvious idea is to use SPACE as the representation of a pause in the TUNE string, and specify its length in the normal way in the rhythm string.

To extend the range of the length values, while preserving their representation by single tokens, it is necessary to use seven tokens in addition to the digit-tokens: '1' to '9'. Obvious candidates are the letters 'a' to 'g', so that 'a' represents 1Ø, 'b' represents 11 and so on – with 'g' representing 16.

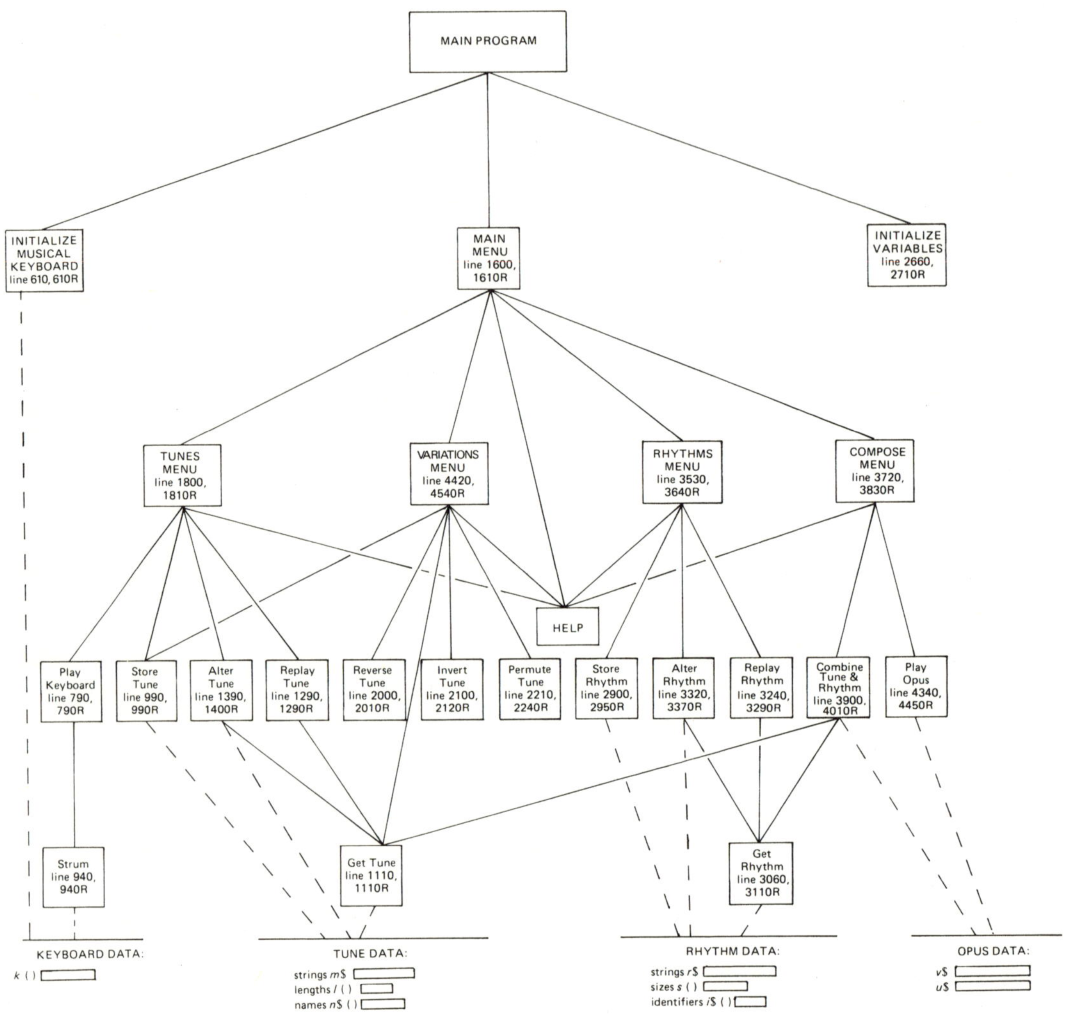

Structure diagram for the MUSIC PROGRAM

When playing a tune, we need to test for the occurrence of **SPACE** because then the program can use the **PAUSE** instruction instead of **BEEP**. It seems a good idea to use a special value for **SPACE**, say 1000, just as we used a special value for it and **ENTER** of −999 before this proposed modification.

But what parts of the program will need changing?

Here is where the structure diagram proves its value.

The data that is affected by the changes can be seen by looking at the diagram, and obviously, the subroutines which actually use that data are the ones which may need changing. It is easy to refer to the diagram and list these:

data	**subroutines**
keyboard data . . . *k*( )	initialize musical keyboard play keyboard strum replay tune
tune strings . . . *m*$	store tune replay tune get tune alter tune
rhythm strings . . . *r*$	store rhythm replay rhythm get rhythm alter rhythm
opus . . . *u*$( ), *v*$( )	play opus combine tune and rhythm

Not all of these subroutines necessarily need any change. It is fairly easy to spot a number of them that don't need changing.

store tune
get tune
alter tune
get rhythm
combine tune and rhythm

The reason none of these need changing is that, none of them attempt to interpret the data, they merely move it about. Consequently, it does not matter to them what the data means. It is when we come to those subroutines which 'unravel' the *meaning* from the data that we have to make changes to allow for the new meanings and representations we are introducing.

For example, every subroutine that includes a BEEP instruction will probably need change because we have to detect the 'notes' whose pitch is apparently 1000, i.e. the SPACE-tokens in the TUNE strings. That applies to

play keyboard
strum
replay tune
play opus

The change in the role of the SPACE-token means that also

initialize musical keyboard

will need modification, to change the look-up table value for SPACE.

The remaining group of subroutines:

store rhythm
alter rhythm
replay rhythm

are all affected by changes in representing the durations of notes. Both *store rhythm* and *alter rhythm* have to check that only valid data is entered by the user, and valid data is now a different set of tokens, namely, the string

"123456789abcdefg"

The *replay rhythm* subroutine needs changing because it has to translate each of these characters into a number.

The changes themselves are not very great. Nor are they difficult to make. The only difficulty is in determining whereabouts such changes need to be made. But, as we have shown, this too is easy, provided the program is cleanly structured and there is a clear, structure diagram to which we can refer.

The actual modifications

(1) In set up musical keyboard subroutine, change the second sub-statement in line 710, so that it reads:

```
700  LET k(13) = –999: LET k(32) = 1000: REM enter & space codes
```

(2) In *play keyboard* subroutine, change line 880 to read

```
880  IF c$ = " " THEN GO TO 820
```

(3) In the *strum* subroutine, there is actually nothing to change because it is called only from *play-keyboard*, which now ignores SPACE.

(4) In the *replay tune* subroutine, insert the line

```
1325 IF a$(z) = " " THEN PAUSE(5Ø*Ø.35) : GO TO 1360
```

The numerical expression used in PAUSE is made up of two factors. The Ø.35 because that is the (arbitrarily chosen) value used in the BEEP instruction in the same subroutine on line 1350, and the factor 5Ø, because BEEP expects its duration in seconds, whilst PAUSE expects it in fiftieths of a second.

(5) The *play opus* subroutine will need modifying to deal both with the detection of pauses, and with the translating of duration value from the rhythm tokens. This second requirement is shared with *replay rhythm*, so the changes to make in *play opus* are to change line 4370 to

```
4370 LET c$ = v$(z): LET duration = CODE c$ – 48: IF c$ >= "a" THEN LET
     duration = duration + 39
```

and insert the line

```
4385 IF pitch = 1000  THEN PAUSE(5*duration): GO TO 4400
```

(6) In *replay rhythms* subroutine, change line 3280 to

```
3280 LET c$ = a$(z): LET duration = CODE c$ – 48: IF c$ >= "a" THEN LET
     duration = duration + 39
```

(7) The string of valid characters tested in *store rhythm* and in *alter rhythm* must be changed

```
2910 LET x$ = "123456789abcdefg"
```

and similarly

```
3325 LET x$ = "123456789abcdefg"
```

A complete *renumbered* version of the MUSIC PROGRAM is provided as Appendix 3.

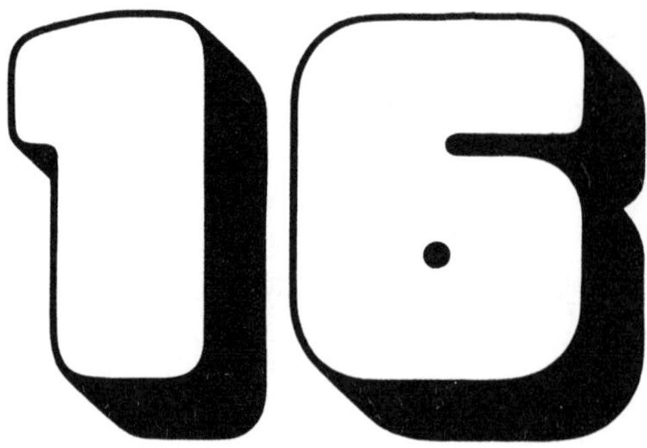

You must know where to draw the line

Straight lines and envelopes

Certain patterns of straight lines produce the impression of curves, even of curved surfaces. Of course, we can exploit this idea to get some interesting patterns on the screen; at the same time we can learn more about the DRAW instruction.

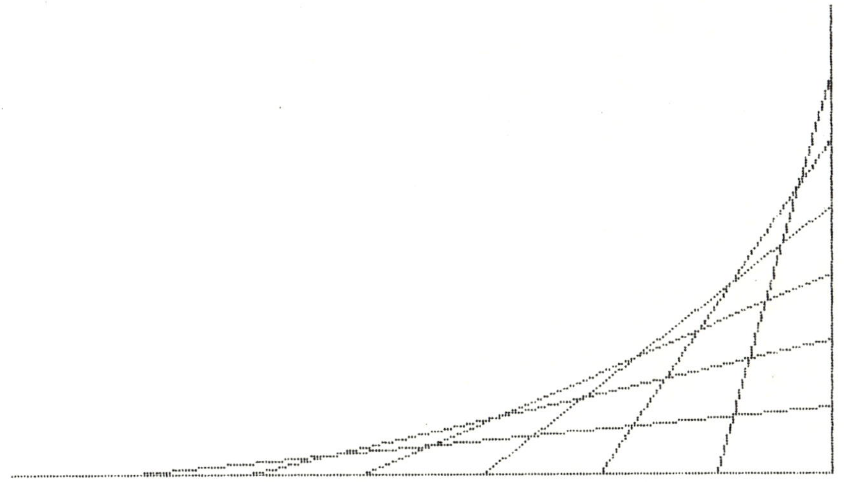

In the example illustration, all the lines are drawn from the bottom edge of the screen to the right-hand edge of the screen. These two edges have been divided into equal intervals, and the start and finish of each line moves along one interval at a time. As a matter of fact, you can make a similar patterns by knocking pins into a board and using string, stretched round the pins, to make straight lines. However, let's take a look at how to program the example illustration.

Using DRAW – Relative Position

The DRAW instruction uses the idea of relative position, so you need to understand how that works. Relative position is similar to relative velocity. If you are in a car going at 50 m.p.h. and another car is going in the same direction at 65 m.p.h., then the second car overtakes you and moves past at a speed that appears to you to be 15 m.p.h., the difference between your two speeds. That's relative velocity. If the fast car was going in the opposite direction its velocity would be negative (because of the opposite direction). So the relative velocity would be

$$((-65) -50) \text{ m.p.h.}$$

i.e., -115 m.p.h.

Any quantity, like velocity, which has direction as well as magnitude, can be looked at from a relative point of view, that is, from the point of view of some observer who has a velocity of his own.

It's the same with position. If you live 5 miles west of town and your friend lives 6 miles west of town, then the position of your friend's house, relative to yours is 6 – 5 miles west. Relative position is equal to Absolute Position minus the Position you start from.

So, when using DRAW, if you want to draw a line that starts at a screen position given by (*xstart, ystart*) and finishes at a new position (*xfin, yfin*), then first you fix your starting position, by plotting a point at it, with the instruction

PLOT xstart, ystart

and then you draw a line to the new (relative) position by

DRAW xfin − xstart, yfin − ystart

Now we can get down to the program to draw the pattern we want.

What do we have to do?

1. Define the limits of x and y, as determined by the frame boundaries.
2. Calculate the intervals along the edge of the frame for x and y
3. Have a loop for dealing with each line. Inside the loop, we
   (a) calculate the start and finish position of the line;
   (b) draw the line

We'll use variables *xf, xl, yf, yl* for the first and last (extreme possible) values of x and y imposed by the limits of the screen; and we'll use n for the number of intervals along each edge. When we calculate the lengths of the intervals, we'll call those *xstep* and *ystep*; and we'll use (*xstart, ystart*) and (*xfin, yfin*) for the starting and finishing points of each line.

Drawing the line

Each line goes from bottom edge to right edge of the frame. So *xfin* and *ystart* are the same for every line. But each time we draw a new line

xstart	increases by *xstep*
yfin	increases by *ystep*

So for each line, the start and finish values required are:

line number	xstart	ystart	xfin	yfin
0	*xf*	*yf*	*xl*	*yf*
1	*xf* + *xstep*	*yf*	*xl*	*yf* + *ystep*
2	*xf* + 2**xstep*	*yf*	*xl*	*yf* + 2**ystep*
.				
.				
.				
k	*xf* + *k***xstep*	*yf*	*xl*	*yf* + *k***ystep*
.				
.				
.				
n	*xf* + *n***xstep*	*yf*	*xl*	*yf* + *n***ystep*

(note that $yf + n*ystep = yl$)

Now we are ready to write the pieces of program corresponding to the list headed 'What do we have to do?' And here they are, followed by their output.

```
1000>REM define frame boundaries
1010 LET xf=0: LET yf=0
1020 LET xl=255: LET yl=175
1030
1040 REM calculate xstep, ystep
1050 INPUT "How many intervals ? ";n
1060 LET xstep=(xl-xf)/n
1070 LET ystep=(yl-yf)/n
1080 LET xfin=xl: LET ystart=yf
1085
1090 REM loop for n+1 lines
1100 FOR k=0 TO n
1110 LET kxstep=k*xstep: LET kystep=k*ystep
1115
1130 LET xstart=INT (0.5+xf+kxstep)
1140 LET yfin=INT (0.5+ystart+kystep)
1150 GO SUB 1500: REM draw line
1310 NEXT k
1315
1320 PRINT "To rerun hit CONT": STOP : CLS : GO TO
 1000
1495
1500 REM draw line SUBR
1510 PLOT xstart,ystart
1520 DRAW (xfin-xstart), (yfin-ystart)
1530 RETURN : REM ********************************
```

20 intervals

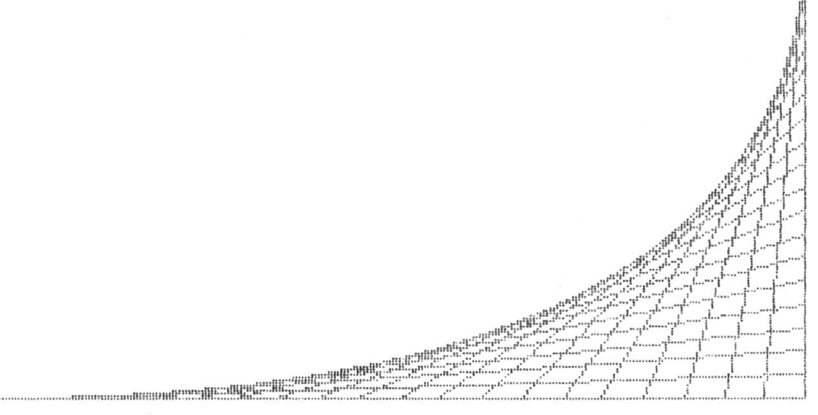

30 intervals

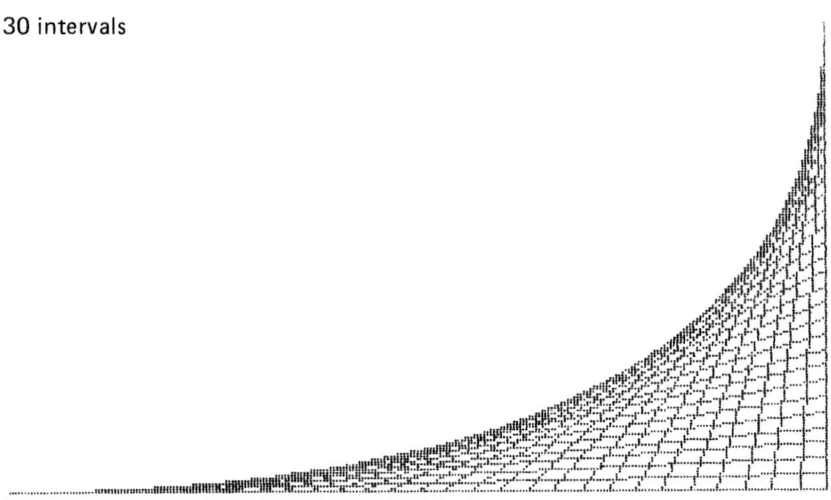

Did you notice something about lines 1120 and 1130? Before assigning the value

$(xf + k*xstep)$

to *xstart*, we added 0.5 and took the INT. This is advisable for the following reason. The value of *k*xstep* is found by dividing $(xl - xf)$ by *n* and then multiplying by *k*. Computers store only approximate values of numbers which are not integers, so there will sometimes be a small error of approximation. The same kind of thing happens if you divide 10 by 3, using decimals, and a fixed number of digits, say 4, for the answer.

The answer you get is 3.333, and when you multiply this by 3, answer is 9.999 instead of 10. Adding 0.5 and taking the INT of a number makes it equal to the nearest integer, which is what is done in lines 1120 and 1130.

If you want to see the effect of *not* taking the INT precaution, alter the program and see what happens with 8 intervals for example.

As usual, we shall now play around to see how we can make the program slightly cleverer, by making some modifications. How about arranging the same pattern in the other three corners of the frame?

Lines drawn from right edge to top edge

xstart and *yfin* are the same for every line.
xstart = *xl* and *yfin* = *yl*

xfin for first line is *xl*, and for each subsequent line it decreases by *xstep*

ystart for first line is *yf*, and for each subsequent line it increases by *ystep*

Lines drawn from top edge to left edge

xfin = *xf* for every line
ystart = *yl* for every line

xstart for first line is *xl,* decreasing by xstep for each subsequent line

yfin for first line is *yl*, decreasing by ystep for each subsequent line

Lines drawn from left edge to bottom edge

xstart = *xf* for every line
yfin = *yf* for every line

xfin = *xl* for first line, and decreases by *xstep* for each subsequent line

ystart = *yl* for first line, and decrease by *ystep* for each subsequent line

Lines in every corner

If we want all four corners filled, all we need to do to the program is to rewrite the 'loop for n + 1 lines', to include instructions for all four corners instead of just one. We shall have to put lines like 1100 inside the new loop instead of outside, because the 'constant' is different for each corner.

The new complete program is as follows, together with illustrations of typical output on the screen.

```
1000>REM define frame boundaries
1010 LET xf=0: LET yf=0
1020 LET xl=255: LET yl=175
1030
1040 REM calculate xstep, ystep
1050 INPUT "How many intervals ? ";n
1060 LET xstep=(xl-xf)/n
1070 LET ystep=(yl-yf)/n
1080
1090 REM loop for n+1 lines
1100 FOR k=0 TO n
1110 LET kxstep=k*xstep: LET kystep=k*ystep
1115
1120 LET xfin=xl: LET ystart=yf
1130 LET xstart=INT (0.5+xf+kxstep)
1140 LET yfin=INT (0.5+ystart+kystep)
1150 GO SUB 1500: REM draw line
1160
1170 LET xstart=xl: LET yfin=yl
```

Listing continued next page

```
1180 LET xfin=INT (0.5+xl-kxstep)
1190 LET ystart=INT (0.5+yf+kystep)
1200 GO SUB 1500: REM draw line 2
1210
1220 LET xfin=xf: LET ystart=yl
1230 LET xstart=INT (0.5+xl-kxstep)
1240 LET yfin=INT (0.5+yl-kystep)
1250 GO SUB 1500: REM draw line 3
1260
1270 LET xstart=xf: LET yfin=yf
1280 LET xfin=INT (0.5+xf+kxstep)
1290 LET ystart=INT (0.5+yl-kystep)
1300 GO SUB 1500: REM draw line 4
1310 NEXT k
1315
1320 PRINT "To rerun hit CONT": STOP : CLS : GO TO
 1000
1495
1500 REM draw line SUBR
1510 PLOT xstart,ystart
1520 DRAW (xfin-xstart), (yfin-ystart)
1530 RETURN : REM *********************************
```

20 intervals

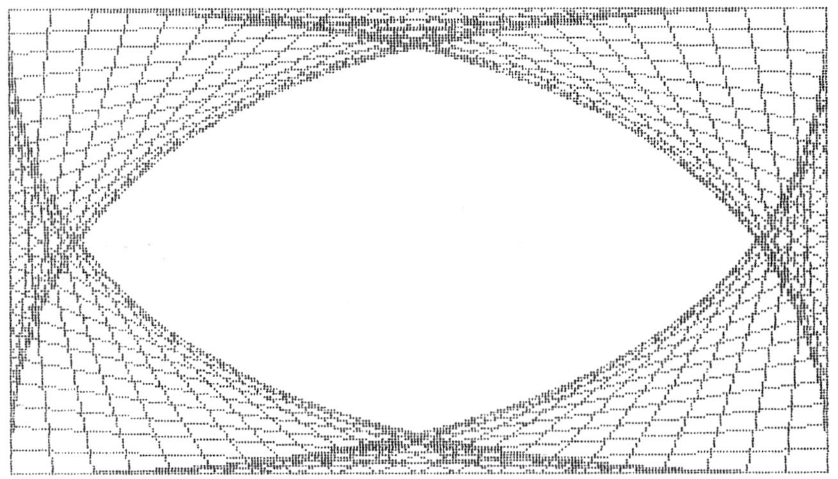

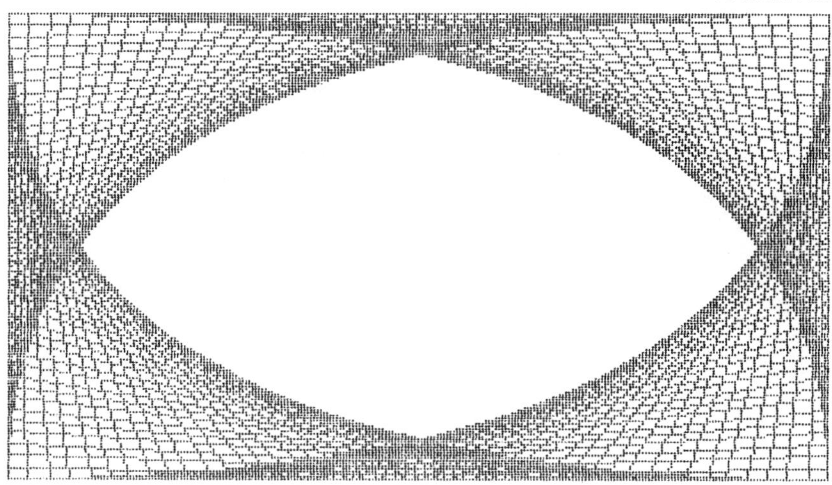

Throwing new light on lampshades

Did you know that the ZX Spectrum is capable of making lampshades for you? Well, pictures of lampshades anyway. Curved lampshades made out of straight lines of course.

This program introduces nothing new except the idea. We know how to plot points around the circumference of an ellipse. We know how to join a point on one ellipse to a point on another ellipse, using DRAW. To get the 'curved surface' effect, one ellipse needs to be twisted round a bit relative to the other. We can do this by offsetting the 'corresponding point' on the second ellipse. Program and illustrations of output below.

This program could do with knocking into better shape, so that the user can input the aspect ratio of the ellipses and the size of the xradius. See what you can do, making sure the program will not crash through the lines going off screen, out of range.

And if you like to see lights inside your lampshades, try using BRIGHT yellow INK on black PAPER.

```
1600>REM lampshades program
1610 CLS : INPUT "How many lines ? "; n
1620 LET theta=2*PI/n
1630 LET xradius=100: LET xmid=127
1640 LET ycentre1=22: LET ycentre2=132
1650 LET yradius=0.1*xradius
1660 INPUT "twist offset ? "; t
1665
1670 FOR k=1 TO n
1680 LET ktheta=k*theta
```

Listing continued next page

```
1690 LET jtheta=(k+t)*theta
1700 LET xstart=xmid+xradius*COS ktheta
1710 LET ystart=ycentre1+yradius*SIN ktheta
1720 LET xfin=xmid+0.7*xradius*COS jtheta
1730 LET yfin=ycentre2+yradius*SIN jtheta
1740 PLOT xstart, ystart
1750 DRAW xfin-xstart, yfin-ystart
1760 NEXT k
1770 STOP : GO TO 1600
```

45 lines, offset 15

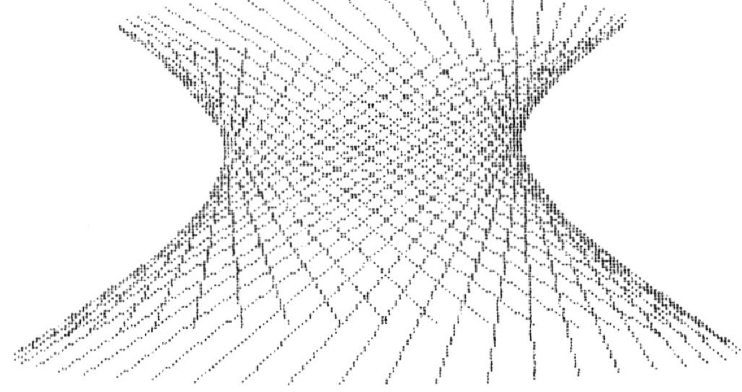

60 lines, offset 15

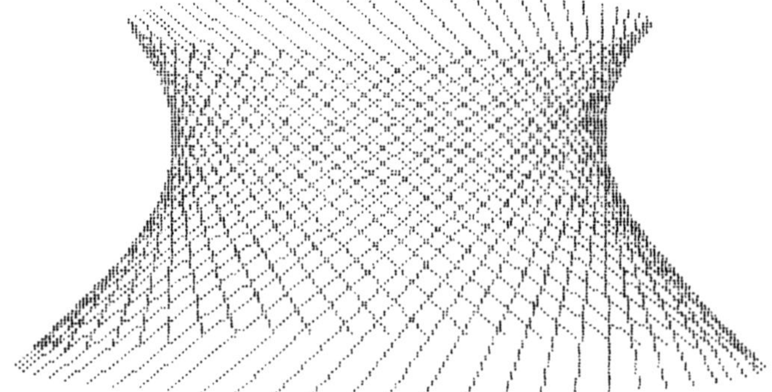

17

Using control codes and defining your own new characters

The code values used by the Specturm are based on the International Standards Organization code. This has a number of National Standard variations, the most widely used being based on an American standard know as ASCII. The ASCII code, or a variant or extension of it is increasingly widely used. This code has 128 values. More and more computers are now using codes which have 256 values, as does the Spectrum, and ASCII code forms a subset of it.

In both ASCII and Spectrum, the first 32 code values, that is, values 0 to 31, are used for non-printable tokens whose function is to control or cause some action when sent from the computer to an external device such as the screen, or a printer. Be warned, however, that, although variations of ASCII are widely used, so that it is a standard in practice as well as in theory, the area in which there is least standardization in practice is the set of interpretations given to the control codes.

One of these control tokens has already been used a number of times in earlier chapters of this book, namely code 13, which is the control code for newline. It is generated by the ENTER key. However, as we have already seen (in Chapter 7), you cannot, for example, include this token in a string by pressing the ENTER key. This is because the computer recognizes it as a control code, and therefore instead of including it in the string being entered, it *interprets* it to mean end-of-line.

That is the feature which distinguishes control codes from codes for printable tokens. Computers and computing equipment are, after all, only our slaves. They have been strictly trained to give special treatment to VIPs, i.e. to control characters. These are not shunted about like the common herd of printable tokens. As soon as one arrives, one can imagine the computer bowing low in utter deference, and saying

'Your wish is my command'
'What is it to be ? . . .

Newline?
Move print position as when using AT ?
Move print position as when using COMMA ?
Backspace ?
Change colour of INK for screen ?
Change colour of PAPER for screen ?
Set FLASH on/off ?
Set BRIGHT on/off ?
Set INVERSE on/off ?
Set OVER on/off ?
Use TAB ?

There is a code for each of these controls, and it must not be confused with the code for the corresponding printable token-name (where this exists). For example, the token-name INK is printable, and its code value is 217. But the control character for ink has the code value 16. If you enter and run

```
100 PRINT INK 4; "green ink"
```

it means exactly the same and does the same as

```
110 PRINT CHR$ 16;CHR$ 4; "green ink"
```

On the other hand

```
120 PRINT CHR$ 217;4; "green ink"
```

does *not* mean the same. Its effect is to print

INK 4 green ink

because the character with code value 217 is the printable token 'INK'.

A more useful variant of line 110, is:

```
130 PRINT CHR$ 16 + CHR$ 4 + "green ink"
```

The reason it is more useful is that the expression to be printed is a valid string expression, which can be assigned to a string variable

```
140 LET a$ = CHR$ 16 + CHR$ 4 + "green ink"
```

Any time you want to print this string (complete with colour), all you need to say is

```
PRINT a$
```

This can be quite useful for a particular string you want to print in several places in a program. Or you can go even further, and store a number of substrings which can be 'glued' together to form a string expression. For example, suppose you want to display the word 'rainbow' frequently in a program, and you would like to print each letter in a different INK-PAPER combination. There is no need to enter the whole string laboriously changing INK and PAPER before each letter. You can get the computer to do the hard work by a few lines such as

```
800 LET x$ = CHR$ 19 + CHR$ 1
810 LET a$ = "rainbow"
820 FOR z = 1 TO 7
830 LET x$ = x$ + CHR$ 16 + CHR$ z
              + CHR$ 17 + CHR$ (7–z)
              + a$(z)
840 NEXT z
```

The meanings of the control characters on the right-hand sides of lines 800 and 830 are as follows:

CHR$ 19 + CHR$ 1	means BRIGHT 1
CHR$ 16 + CHR$ z	means PAPER z
CHR$ 17 + CHR$ (7–z)	means INK 7–z

The complete list of control characters which can be used in a similar way, by embedding them in strings, is:

control code	effect
6	same as COMMA in a PRINT list
8	backspace
13	newline
16	INK
17	PAPER
18	FLASH
19	BRIGHT
20	INVERSE
21	OVER
22	AT
23	TAB

User-defined graphics

In addition to the square blob mosaic patterns on keytops '1' to '8' (in GRAPHIC mode), you can define your own graphic characters quite easily.

Each character is defined by a square of 8 × 8 dots on the screen. Think of this as 8 rows of 8 dots. Each row can be represented by a sequence of zeros and ones – '1' for when the dot is INK colour, and '0' for when the dot is PAPER colour.

Each sequence of this kind must be preceded by the keyword 'BIN', whether it is input from the keyboard, included in a DATA statement, or included in program.

The computer has space reserved for storing user-defined graphics in its memory, and these graphics can be retrieved by using the keytops marked with the letter 'a' through the alphabet to 'u'. In order to store the eight BIN patterns required to define a particular graphic, you can choose any one of those keytops for it. Then you need to use two special functions. One of these is POKE, which we have already used, though not many times (see Chapter 9). The other is USR. The expression

USR "a"

gives the address in computer memory of the byte used to store the first row, or BIN pattern, of the user-defined graphic to be assigned to keytop 'a'. The address for storing the:

second byte is .... USR "a" + 1
third byte is .... USR "a" + 2
. .
. .
. .
eighth byte is .... USR "a" + 7

The way POKE works, you may remember, is that it must be followed by an address, then a comma, and then a value which it will poke into the address. To define a complete user-defined graphic therefore needs eight POKE instructions. Of course these can be in a loop, in which a READ statement reads each BIN pattern from a DATA statement.

For example suppose we want to define a graphic with the pattern of the oblique stroke, '\', and store it where it will be retrieved by using keytop 's' (in graphics mode). The following program will do it. First come the DATA statements, then the loop that reads each one and pokes it into the appropriate address, using USR.

```
100 DATA BIN 1 0 0 0 0 0 0 0
110 DATA BIN 0 1 0 0 0 0 0 0
120 DATA BIN 0 0 1 0 0 0 0 0
130 DATA BIN 0 0 0 1 0 0 0 0
140 DATA BIN 0 0 0 0 1 0 0 0
150 DATA BIN 0 0 0 0 0 1 0 0
160 DATA BIN 0 0 0 0 0 0 1 0
170 DATA BIN 0 0 0 0 0 0 0 1
180 FOR r = 0 TO 7
190 READ row pattern
200 POKE USR "s" + r, row pattern
210 NEXT r
220 PRINT "s"
230 STOP
```

As you see, the program finishes by printing the newly defined graphic. But that is not all. Once you have run the program, enter the command, LIST. You will find that the program looks slightly different. Furthermore, every time you press the 's' keytop in graphics mode, and ENTER it, you will get the oblique stroke instead of capital 'S'.

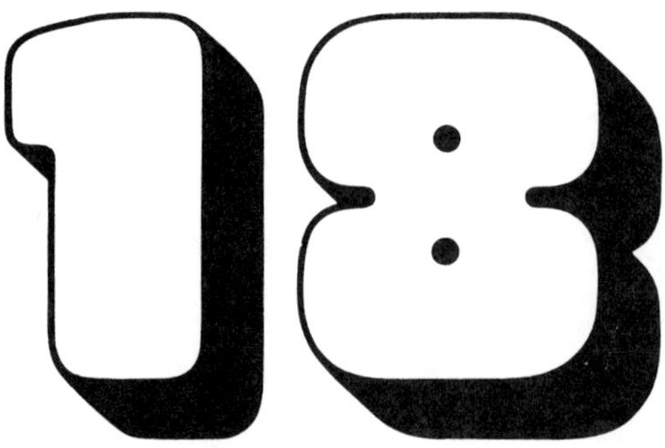

What is a good programming language?

By now, you should be quite familiar with BASIC as a programming language. Having learned how to use it to do all kinds of things, perhaps you now take it for granted as THE-WAY-YOU-TALK-TO-A-COMPUTER. Nothing could be further from the truth.

If we were to look deeply into the inner workings of the computer, we should find that it doesn't understand BASIC at all. It doesn't *understand* anything as a matter of fact, any more than a washing machine *understands* its washing program. Part of the memory of the computer is called ROM, which stand for Read-Only-Memory. That means you can't change what is stored in it by writing new information to it. The ROM contains all the programs which make the computer spring to life as soon as you switch it on. One of these programs processes the stream of characters which make up the BASIC PROGRAMS you enter, and *interprets* them into actions (just like the washing machine). A program that does this is called an INTERPRETER.

Every BASIC line of your program is running, before the appropriate action is taken. Not every system running BASIC works like this. An alternative method is to have the system use a program which *translates BASIC programs into machine-code* – a series of electrical pulses stored in a form which we can represent as sequences of noughts and ones, and called BINARY. A translator program which does this is called a COMPILER. You can see that using a compiler, you would have to work in two stages

Stage 1 . . . translate BASIC into machine-code
Stage 2 . . . RUN machine-code program

Once you have the translated machine-code program, it is translated once and for all, and you can run it as many times as you wish. When it is run, since there is no translating involved, it runs very, very much faster than would the original BASIC program using an interpreter.

So, from the point of view of speed, a compiler is superior to an interpreter. However, the main disadvantage for a small system is that it requires much greater memory space in which to store the translated machine-code program produced.

There are other important difference too, between interpreters and compilers. However, the point I really want to expand is that, regardless of whether your computer uses an interpreter or a compiler program there is a wide choice of programming languages other than BASIC, which can be interpreted or compiled.

For small computers, the BASIC language has become very widely used for *two* reasons:

(1) A BASIC INTERPRETER program takes comparatively little store and is easy to write
(2) The initial stages of learning BASIC are very easy, so it helps the manufacturers to sell their computers to *new* computer users, people who have never before used a computer.

However, for writing a non-trivial program, that is a program of any size or complexity, BASIC is very far from being an ideal language. Let us take a look at some of the problems we had to overcome in putting together the MUSIC PROGRAM and see how we were forced, by the limits of the BASIC language, to use clumsy solutions.

Out of the several hundred programming languages in use by professional programmers, there is *no* best language. Each has its disadvantages. Some also have advantages! One which has gained in popularity, and is now widely available on almost all micros, is the language called PASCAL. The main purpose of this chapter is, not to teach you to use PASCAL, but to give you a basis for understanding the important differences between it and BASIC.

The important differences between languages have little to do with their appearance, and very much to do with the programming structures and the data structures which they provide ready-made. Then there are the rules controlling the way names used in programs are handled – names for data, names of instructions (line-numbers in BASIC), names of subroutines. Then again, there are mechanisms which handle the interfacing between subroutines and main program – making it easier to pass information back and forth between them. We'll start by taking a look at this last point.

Interfacing Subroutines – Parameters

First of all, what is meant by the word 'parameter'? It is a very useful word because it carries such a useful meaning. When you use the CIRCLE instruction in BASIC, you are, effectively, using a system-provided subroutine whose *name* is CIRCLE. This subroutine requires three pices of data (the *x*-coordinate and *y*-coordinate of the centre, and the radius). These three pieces of data are called the *parameters* of CIRCLE.

If you wish to write a BASIC subroutine that needs three such parameters, you have to decide to set aside three variables for this purpose, and *always use the same three variables,* because the subroutine always expects to find the values it wants, stored in these variables. Not so with CIRCLE – you can use *any* three variables. Or you need not use variables as such, but expressions giving the required values. All the following are valid uses of CIRCLE:

```
CIRCLE x, y, z
CIRCLE a, b, c
CIRCLE 80, 95, 10
CIRCLE COS(x*y – 3*a + 24), 24, b
```

In the MUSIC PROGRAM, there were several occasions when we had to *duplicate* a subroutine, making changes *only* to its interface, when what we really needed was the same subroutine with different parameters! A glaring example is the pair of subroutines *get tune* and *get rhythm* (see full program in Appendix 3, lines 1110–1280, and 3110–3280). These two subroutines are almost identical. We can list the differences. In each case it is a question of data values

get tune	**get rhythm**
"tune"	"rhythm"
no of tunes	*no of rhythms*
n$( )	*i*$( )
l( )	*s*( )
m$	*r*$

If we were using PASCAL instead of BASIC, we should have used the *same* subroutine, and it would have had five parameters, one for each of the pieces of data which can be different each time the subroutine is used. In PASCAL, subroutines can be given alphabetic names, like variables, not just line-numbers. So we might call this subroutine *GET STRING*, and when we used it, it would be followed by the list of parameters to be passed to it, enclosed in brackets, e.g., something like

GET STRING ("tune", no of tunes, n$, 1, m$)

or

GET STRING ("rhythm", no of rhythms, i$, s, r$)

Furthermore, it could be used unchanged in a lot of other programs, giving it a different set of suitable parameters. This is just what happens when you use DEF FN and FN in BASIC, where you *can* pass paramters. Unfortunately, in BASIC, a user-defined function FN, can only be defined by a *single* statement which is, effectively, a statement like a LET statement. Being able to pass parameters to a subroutine is a tremendous step forward in comparison. In PASCAL there are two kinds of subroutine, those which are FUNCTIONS and another kind, called PROCEDURES. Just as in BASIC, functions are things that you can include in an expression, like INT or LEN or CHR$. The procedures are the subroutines you can't use that way, because it wouldn't make sense – they don't have values – just like CIRCLE or PRINT in BASIC.

In the MUSIC PROGRAM, we have many semi-duplicated subroutines, which, in PASCAL, could be single procedures. The resulting program would be very, very much shorter in PASCAL than in BASIC, and would require much less effort both to write it and to organize the interfacing of its parts.

The next important language difference we'll look at is also connected with subroutines.

Names and Meanings

Humpty Dumpty, the egg-head who sat on the wall in Lewis Carroll's looking-glass world, would definitely have preferred PASCAL to BASIC.

'When I use a word',
he said,
'It means what *I* want it to mean !'

If you are writing a subroutine in BASIC, and you happen to use, say, *k* as the control-variable for a loop inside the subroutine, the result can be disastrous if it just so happens that you call the subroutine from inside a loop in main program which is also using *k* as its control-variable. Obviously, you want the *k* inside the subroutine to mean something quite different from the *k* in main program. However, if you do this in BASIC, your program is likely to fall off the wall, and all the king's horses and all the king's men, will not be able to put it together again, unless they have done a *crash* course in programming!

In PASCAL, by contrast, when *you* use a variable name, *you* decide what it means. You can decide to make it mean a *different* variable inside a subroutine, or the *same* one as outside, whichever you want; but this does result in your being required to define what your variable names mean, in special statements called *declarations.* (In BASIC, the DIM statement is a declaration – it defines the named variable to be an array and specifies its dimensions.)

The ability to seal off the inner workings of a PASCAL subroutine by using names which are private to it, means that it is easy to write them in such a way that they may be safely used in any program without fears of unforeseen interaction resulting from name confusion.

Another difference about names, which, although comparatively minor, is certainly helpful in writing clear programs, is that none of the names used in PASCAL are restricted to being a single letter, so you can choose meaningful names for all your variables, not just some of them, whether they are numeric, character, or arrays.

The third major difference between PASCAL and BASIC is PASCAL's relative abundance of different *types* of data.

Data Types and Data Structures

In BASIC, there are basically two types of data, *numeric* and *character-string.* And BASIC has just two kinds of data structure. Its atomic structure is the simple variable. Its only other structure is the array.

PASCAL provides several different types of simple values. Among these it distinguishes *two* numerical types, one called *integer,* and the other called *real.* PASCAL *integer* values are always exact, and can be safely used for counting, whereas its real values, like numeric values generally in BASIC, are approximations, and have fractional parts. It also has a type (called *boolean*) whose value can only be one of two possibilities TRUE or FALSE. Expressions like

$$x > y$$

whose value is either TRUE or FALSE, may be assigned to a variable of boolean type, and this turns out to be a very useful thing. There are other, more exotic, *types* which we shall not go into here, but their existence certainly contributes to the power of the language, and the ease with which a programmer is able to define complex systems.

In addition to *arrays,* one can in PASCAL define data structures called *records.* These make it easier to use data-names which clearly express the relations linking different pieces of data. For example, in the MUSIC PROGRAM we used a string *m$* to store tunes, an array *n$( )* for the names of the tunes, and an array *l( )* for their lengths. It would be possible in PASCAL to use a *record,* which included the name of a tune, its length, and the tune itself in separate parts of the record. You can refer to a whole record by the record name, or you can refer to a particular part of it by following the record name with a dot and then the name of the part wanted. For example, if the name of the record is *tune* and the names of its separate parts are *name, length* and *notes,* then we can refer to:

tune.name,
tune.length, or
tune.notes

as we wish.

We can also, of course, have an array of such records, or include an array as part of a record. Further, it is possible to define a record-structure of any kind you like giving the *type of structure* itself a *name,* and then to declare variable-names which are of that type simply by mentioning the name of the type together with the name of the variable.

Operating systems

If you become interested enough in programming to want to learn another language, such as PASCAL, you will find that the programming language itself is not the only thing that makes life heaven or hell for the programmer.

Equally, or perhaps even more important, is the ease with which you can save and load programs from some secondary kind of memory. From this point of view, cassette is not satisfactory. Not only is it slow, but you have to be your own filing clerk. A good computer operating system provides you with a filing system for the programs and data you want to save. It arranges their safe keeping, keeps a directory of files you have saved, and finds them for you with no trouble on your part, and with a minimum of delay. It then becomes very easy to modify files, keep several versions of the same file, and to link together, into one program, subroutines kept in several files.

The most commonly used cheap memory device for this kind of operation is currently the floppy disk. The disks themselves are as cheap as cassettes, but the disk drives are a factor of ten times the price of a cassette recorder. Of course this may change. At the time of writing, so-called 'micro-drives' have been announced for this computer, at a price which, though dearer than cassette recorders, makes the micro-drives sound an extremely attractive buy, provided they fulfil the promises made for their technical performance.

Another important feature of a programming language is the ease with which you can use it to carry out computer operations which are not always part of a program. Here BASIC scores over PASCAL. Operations like SAVE and LOAD and VERIFY don't exist in PASCAL, and you would have to use special commands *outside* your PASCAL program to carry out such operations. The fact that they *do* exist *inside* BASIC makes it possible to automate some of the tricky operations involved when, for example, using cassettes. As an example of this see the SAVE and VERIFY PROGRAM which is included as Appendix 1.

I would not recommend trying to use PASCAL on a cassette-based system. But if the micro-drives are successful, then the way is open to progress, with this computer, from more earthbound BASIC computing to the new programming space of PASCAL.

Appendices

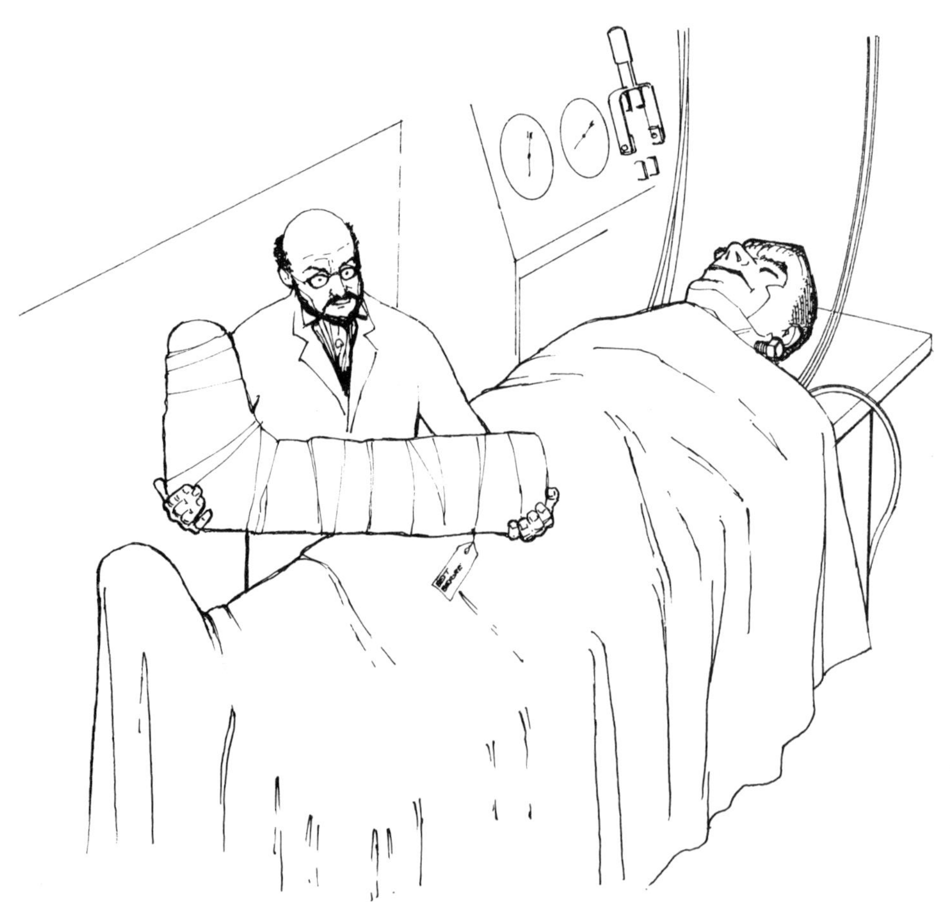

SAVE AND VERIFY PROGRAM 1

```
1990>REM ****************************************
TO SAVE AND VERIFY YOUR PROGRAM AND ITS VARIABLES
Add the following lines to any program. When you w
ant to SAVE it, just enter RUN 2000.  If you want
to SAVE the variables as well as the program, ente
r GO TO 2000 instead.
```

```
2000 REM save & verify program
2020 CLS : INPUT "SAVING on cassette"'"Enter PROGR
AM-NAME.",z$
2030 PRINT '"SAVING on cassette"''''''"1. Plug in m
ic."''''"2.Unplug earphone."''''"3.Start cassette on
 RECORD."''''"4.ENTER CONTINUE.": STOP
2050 SAVE z$
2060 CLS : PRINT  FLASH 1;"SAVE COMPLETED"''''; BRI
GHT 1; INVERSE 1;"STOP TAPE"
2070 PRINT ''''"and then ENTER CONTINUE"
2073 BEEP 0.2,36: BEEP 0.2,0
2074 BEEP 0.2,36: BEEP 0.2,0
2075 BEEP 0.2,36: BEEP 0.2,0
2076 BEEP 0.2,36: BEEP 0.2,0
2077 BEEP 0.2,36: BEEP 0.2,0: STOP
2080 CLS : PRINT "NOW VERIFY"''''''"1.Rewind the Ta
pe."''''"2.Unplug the mic."''''"3.Plug in the earpho
ne."''''"4.Start the Tape on PLAY."''''"5.ENTER CONT
INUE .": STOP
2090 PRINT ''"VERIFY started.": VERIFY z$: CLS : P
RINT "VERIFYDONE"''''"STOP the tape and REWIND."
2100 STOP
```

2 KEYTOPS AND CORRESPONDING MUSICAL NOTES, USING THE MUSIC PROGRAM MUSICAL KEYBOARD

SIX OCTAVES OF KEYTOPS						Basic pitch	MUSICAL NOTE
1	e	g	!	>=	THEN	6	F
2	r	h	@	<	^	7	F sharp, G flat
3	t	j	£	>	-	8	G
4	y	k	$	AND	+	9	G sharp, A flat
5	u	l	%	OR	=	10	A
6	i	z	&	AT	:	11	A sharp, B flat
7	o	x	'	;	`	0	C
8	p	c	(	"	?	1	C sharp, D flat
9	a	v	)	STOP	/	2	D
0	s	b	_	NOT	*	3	D sharp, E flat
q	d	n	<=	STEP	,	4	E
w	f	m	<>	TO	.	5	E sharp, F flat

3 THE MUSIC PROGRAM – COMPLETE LISTING

```
 500>REM          ...MAIN PROGRAM...
 510 RESTORE
 520 FOR z=1 TO 13: READ y: BEEP 0.1,y: NEXT z
 530 DATA 0,4,7,12,14,12,14,12,14,12,7,4,0
 540 CLS : PRINT ''TAB 13;"WELCOME"'';TAB 6;"TO TH
E MUSIC PROGRAM"''''"           No smoking please "'''
"  There will be a short delay"'"  while the micro
-harpsichord"'"  is assembled and tuned, and"'"  t
he stops are bored in the"'"  micro-flute."''''"IF
YOU WANT TO KNOW HOW TO USE"'"THIS PROGRAM CHOOSE
'HELP' WHEN"'"THE MAIN MENU IS DISPLAYED."
 550 GO SUB 2710: REM init line-nos
 560 GO SUB 0610: REM keyboard
 570 RESTORE : FOR z=1 TO 6: READ pitch: LET durat
ion=3: GO SUB 950: NEXT z
 575 GO SUB 6000: REM sig opus
 580 GO SUB 1610: REM Main Menu
 590 STOP : RETURN
 600 REM end of main program
```

```
 610 REM ******** init mus keyboard SUBR *********
 620 DIM k(255)
 630 FOR j=1 TO 255: LET k(j)=999: NEXT j
 640 LET s$="1234567890qwertyuiopasdfghjklzxcvbnm"
: REM all the keytops in keyboard order
 650 LET s$=s$+"!@£$%&'()_<=<>>=<> AND  OR AT ;""
STOP NOT  STEP  TO  THEN ^-+=:`?/*,.": REM ditto w
ith SYMBOL SHIFT
 660 LET bottom p=-18: LET top p=bottom p+(LEN s$-
1)
 670 FOR j=1 TO LEN s$
```

Listing continued next page

```
 680 LET pitch=bottom p +j-1
 690 LET k(CODE s$(j))=pitch
 700 NEXT j
 710 LET k(13)=-999: LET k(32)=1000: REM enter & s
pace codes
 720 REM ********** set up strum chords **********
 730 DIM h(4)
 740 DATA 0,4,7,12
 750 RESTORE 0740
 760 FOR z=1 TO 4: READ h(z)
 770 NEXT z
 780 RETURN : REM ****** end of subroutine *******


 790 REM ********** play-keyboard SUBR ***********
 800 CLS : PRINT "The keyboard"'"is now a musical
keyboard."'"Start Playing !"'''"The  SPACE  key ca
n be used to"'"indicate a (silent) pause."'''"When
 you have picked out a tune you want to store, wri
te it downbefore you return to the"'"TUNES Menu."'
''"To return to  menu, hit ENTER."
 810 REM wait till NO finger ON
 820 LET c$=INKEY$
 830 IF c$<>"" THEN  GO TO 0820
 840 REM wait till ONE finger ON
 850 LET c$=INKEY$
 860 IF c$="" THEN  GO TO 0850
 870 IF c$=CHR$ 13 THEN  GO TO 0930
 880 IF c$=" " THEN  GO TO 820
 890 LET pitch=k(CODE c$)
 900 LET duration=1
 910 GO SUB 950: REM strum
 920 GO TO 820
 930 RETURN : REM ****** end of subroutine *******


 940 REM *********** strum SUBRoutine ************
```

```
 950 FOR d=1 TO duration
 960 FOR Y=1 TO 4: BEEP .02,h(Y)+pitch: NEXT Y
 970 NEXT d
 980 RETURN : REM ********************************

 990 REM ************ store tune SUBr ************
1000 INPUT "Enter token string "'"of tune to be st
ored."'"If no tune to store, hit ENTER   ",a$
1010 IF a$="" THEN  RETURN
1020 REM next line is entry point when a$ is alrea
dy stored, BUT NOT b$
1030 IF no of tunes=max THEN  PRINT "Sorry, too ma
ny tunes."''"enter CONT to continue": STOP : RETUR
N
1040 INPUT "Enter name of new tune."'"If no tune t
o store, hit ENTER   ",b$
1050 IF b$="" THEN  RETURN
1060 LET no of tunes=no of tunes+1: REM Entry poin
t from rhythm & tune data INIT subroutines
1070 LET m$=m$+a$
1080 LET n$(no of tunes)=b$
1090 LET l(no of tunes)=LEN a$
1100 RETURN : REM ********* end of SUBr **********

1110 REM ************* get tune SUBr **************
1120 INPUT " Enter name of tune wanted"'"or if not
hing wanted, hit ENTER",b$
1130 IF b$="" THEN  RETURN
1140 LET start=1
1150 FOR z=LEN b$+1 TO 15: LET b$=b$+" ": NEXT z
1160 FOR z=1 TO no of tunes
1170 IF n$(z)=b$ THEN  LET wanted=z: GO TO 1260
1180 LET start=start+l(z)
1190 NEXT z
```

Listing continued next page

```
1200 CLS : PRINT b$,"   not found"'"**************
**************************************************
"
1210 PRINT "Full list of names stored is"''
1220 FOR z=1 TO no of tunes
1230 PRINT n$(z),l(z);" notes long"
1240 NEXT z: PRINT
1250 GO TO 1120
1260 REM name found
1270 LET a$=m$(start TO start+l(wanted)-1)
1280 PRINT b$,"found"'a$:  RETURN : REM end of get
 tune SUBR ***************************************


1290 REM ********** replay tune SUBr *************
1300 GO SUB 1120: REM get tune
1310 IF b$="" THEN  RETURN
1320 FOR z=1 TO LEN a$
1330 IF a$(z)=" " THEN  PAUSE (50*0.35): GO TO 137
0
1340 LET pitch=k(CODE a$(z))
1350 LET duration=0.35
1360 BEEP duration,pitch
1370 NEXT z
1380 GO TO 1300
1390 RETURN : REM *** end of replay tune SUBr ****


1400 REM ************ alter tune SUBr ************
1410 GO SUB 1120: REM get tune
1420 IF b$="" THEN  RETURN
1430 INPUT "Enter string to be changed."'"If nothi
ng to change, hit ENTER",o$
1440 IF o$="" THEN  RETURN
1450 LET olen=LEN o$
1460 FOR z=start TO start+l(wanted)-olen
1470 LET w=z
```

```
1480 IF o$=m$(w TO w+olen-1) THEN  GO TO 1530: REM
 name found
1490 NEXT z
1500 PRINT o$'"not found"
1510 INPUT "string not found"'"Hit ENTER and try a
gain",q$
1520 GO TO 1430
1530 INPUT "Enter fresh string"'"or hit ENTER to d
elete"'f$
1540 LET t$=m$(start+l(wanted) TO LEN m$): REM tai
l of unaltered tunes stored after in m$
1550 LET h$=m$(start TO w-1)
1560 LET a$=h$+f$+m$(w+olen TO start+l(wanted)-1):
 PRINT ''"Tune is now"''a$
1570 LET m$=m$(1 TO start-1)+a$+t$
1580 LET l(wanted)=l(wanted)+LEN f$-olen: REM new
length of tune stored
1590 GO TO 1430
1600 RETURN : REM **** end of alter tune SUBr ****


1610 REM *********    Main Menu SUBr    *********
1620 LET x$="htvrc STOP ": REM  sequence of menu-
choice tokens
1630 CLS : PRINT '''TAB 9;"music program"';TAB 11;
"MAIN MENU"''
1640 PRINT "Sub-menus available       token"'"....
................       ....."''
1650 PRINT "  HELP (ie info)";TAB 29;"h"''
1660 PRINT "  TUNES";TAB 29;"t"''
1670 PRINT "  VARIATIONS";TAB 29;"v"''
1680 PRINT "  RHYTHMS";TAB 29;"r"''
1690 PRINT "  COMPOSE";TAB 29;"c"''
1700 PRINT "   STOP ";TAB 28;" STOP "
1710 INPUT "CHOOSE SUB-MENU."'"Enter token",c$
```

Listing continued next page

```
1720 REM to main program
1730 FOR z=1 TO LEN x$
1740 LET choice=z
1750 IF c$=x$(z) THEN  GO TO 1780
1760 NEXT z
1770 INPUT "You entered """;CHR$ (CODE c$);""","'"
which is not in the menu."'"Try again",c$: GO TO 1
730
1780 GO SUB c(choice)
1790 GO TO 1620
1800 REM *****  end of Main Menu SUBr ************
```

```
1810 REM       Tunes Menu SUBr     *****************
1820 LET x$="hpsra STOP "
1830 CLS : PRINT '''TAB 9;"music program"';TAB 8;"
TUNES  SUB-MENU"''
1840 PRINT "  choices available        token"'"  .
.................          ....."
1850 PRINT "  HELP (ie info)";TAB 29;"h"''
1860 PRINT "  PLAY KEYBOARD";TAB 29;"p"''
1870 PRINT "  STORE TUNE";TAB 29;"s"''
1880 PRINT "  REPLAY TUNE";TAB 29;"r"''
1890 PRINT "  ALTER TUNE";TAB 29;"a"''
1900 PRINT "  EXIT (return to Main Menu)";TAB 29;"
e"''
1910 PRINT "   STOP ";TAB 28;" STOP "
1920 INPUT "CHOOSE OPTION."'"Enter token",c$
1930 FOR z=1 TO LEN x$
1940 LET choice=z
1950 IF c$=x$(z) THEN  GO TO 1990
1960 NEXT z
1970 IF c$="e" THEN  RETURN
1980 INPUT "You entered """;CHR$ (CODE c$);""","'"
```

```
which is not in the menu."'"Try again",c$: GO TO 1
930
1990 GO SUB c(choice+t offset)
2000 GO TO 1820: REM  end of Tunes Menu SUBr ***



2010 REM ************* reverse SUBr **************
2020 GO SUB 1120: REM get tune
2030 IF b$="" THEN  RETURN
2040 LET len=LEN a$
2050 LET mid=INT (0.1+len/2)
2060 FOR z=1 TO mid
2070 LET k$=a$(z): LET a$(z)=a$(len-z+1): LET a$(l
en-z+1)=k$
2080 NEXT z
2090 PRINT "Tune now reversed."'a$
2100 GO SUB 1030: REM store tune using 2nd entry p
oint
2110 RETURN : REM ******************************

2120 REM *************** inv SUBr ****************
2130 GO SUB 1120: REM get tune
2140 IF b$="" THEN  RETURN
2150 FOR z=1 TO LEN a$
2160 LET oldpz=k(CODE a$(z))
2170 LET newpz=top p-(oldpz-bottom p)
2180 LET position=newpz+1-bottom p
2190 LET a$(z)=s$(position)
2200 NEXT z
2210 PRINT "Tune now inverted."'a$
2220 GO SUB 1030: REM store tune using 2nd entry p
oint
2230 RETURN : REM ******************************
```

Listing continued next page

```
2240 REM ************** perm SUBr *****************
2250 GO SUB 1120: REM get tune
2260 IF b$="" THEN  RETURN
2270 LET len=LEN a$: LET factor=len
2280 FOR z=7 TO 2 STEP -1
2290 IF len=z*INT (len/z) THEN  LET factor=z: GO
TO 2310
2300 NEXT z
2310 REM factor divides len exactly
2320 LET first=1: LET last=factor: LET mid=INT (0.
1+factor/2): LET times=INT (0.1+len/factor)
2330 FOR z=1 TO times
2340 FOR y=first TO mid
2350 LET k$=a$(y): LET a$(y)=a$(last-y+first): LET
 a$(last-y+first)=k$
2360 NEXT y
2370 LET first=first+factor: LET mid=mid+factor: L
ET last=last+factor
2380 NEXT z
2390 PRINT "Tune now permed."'a$
2400 GO SUB 1030: REM store tune using 2nd entry p
oint
2410 RETURN : REM **********************************


2420 REM ******** rhythm & tune data SUBr ********
2430 LET b$="daisy"
2440 LET a$="333311121633331112151111211412121141 2
1212111111216": REM length is 51 chars
2450 GO SUB 3050: REM store rhythm, using 2nd entr
y point
2460 LET a$="xkfoadfafohxkfadfhkhklkhxkhfhkfafaoof
khofkhklxkfhof"
2470 GO SUB 1060: REM store tune, using 3rd entry
point
2480 LET b$="song": REM length  is 94
2490 LET a$="422422422842244422444224224228422 44g4
```

```
224222222442222422222242242242242242242242244"
2500 LET a$=a$+"4224224228422444224442242242244422
44g"
2510 GO SUB 3050: REM store rhythm, using 2nd entr
y point
2520 LET a$="gfggfgzlz!nbcbczljljgfggfgzlz!nxcbczl
mbcjlzcbm!glcmbcjlzcbm!g!!$@!g!!$@!g!!$@!$@!$@!g"
2530 LET a$=a$+"gfggfgzlz!nbcbczljljgfggfgzlz£!nxc
bcz"
2540 GO SUB 1060: REM store tune, using 3rd entry
point
2550 LET b$="zion"
2560 LET a$="2222442222844442222844442222844442222
844442222224444422228"
2570 GO SUB 3050: REM store rhythm, using 2nd entr
y point
2580 LET a$="adfhkklklvkhhffdadfaavvvxvxlkavvvxvxl
khhffhklxkhfhhffdadfa"
2590 GO SUB 1060: REM store tune, using 3rd entry
point
2600 LET b$="irisheyes"
2610 LET a$="2424228114242a11424226224242a24242281
14242a11424264112224 2a": REM length is 59 chars
2620 GO SUB 3050: REM store rhythm, using 2nd entr
y point
2630 LET a$="xkkhfkxkflvmvxvnmnmnvxlkvhhkhxkkhfkxk
flvmvxvnmn@m$xzxvnm@mm"
2640 GO SUB 1060: REM store tune, using 3rd entry
point
2650 LET b$="dickybird"
2660 LET a$="111112131111116321212121111411334111
1121621111212121111113": REM length is 60 chars
2670 GO SUB 3050: REM store rhythm, using 2nd entr
y point
2680 LET a$="hgkhdoytrhkhhhoikakhdaoyddaoadaoaiyro
adfkahfdaokhfahhfdaodhx"
```

Listing continued next page

```
2690 GO SUB 1060: REM store tune, using 3rd entry
point
2700 RETURN : REM ********************************
**************
2710 REM ********** set up initial values and ****
************** subr-line nos SUBr ****************
2720 LET r$="": LET m$="": LET max=20: LET no of r
hythms=0: LET no of tunes=0
2730 DIM c(30): DIM s(max): DIM l(max): DIM i$(max
,15): DIM n$(max,15)
2740 LET t offset=6
2750 LET r offset=t offset+6
2760 LET c offset=r offset+5
2770 LET v offset=c offset+4
2780 RESTORE 2790: REM MAIN MENU     - help, tunes
, variations,      rhythms, compose,  STOP
2790 DATA 4730, 1810, 4540, 3640, 3830, 590
2800 FOR z=1 TO t offset: READ c(z): NEXT z
2810 RESTORE 2820: REM TUNES MENU - help, play-key
board, store, replay, alter,  STOP
2820 DATA 4730,790, 990, 1290, 1400, 590
2830 FOR z=t offset+1 TO r offset: READ c(z): NEXT
 z
2840 RESTORE 2850: REM RHYTHMS MENU - help, store,
 replay, alter,  STOP
2850 DATA 4730, 2950, 3290, 3370, 590
2860 FOR z=r offset+1 TO c offset: READ c(z): NEXT
 z
2870 RESTORE 2880: REM COMPOSE MENU - help, combin
e, play opus, STOP
2880 DATA 4730, 4010, 4450, 590
2890 FOR z=c offset+1 TO v offset: READ c(z): NEXT
 z
2900 RESTORE 2910: REM VARIATIONS MENU - help, rev
erse, invert, perm, STOP
2910 DATA 4730,2010, 2120, 2240, 590
2920 FOR z=v offset+1 TO v offset+5: READ c(z): NE
```

```
XT z
2930 GO SUB 2420: REM rhythm & tunes data
2940 RETURN : REM end of SUBr    ******************

2950 REM *********** store rhythm SUBr ***********
2960 LET x$="123456789abcdefg"
2970 INPUT "Enter token string "'"of rhythm to be
stored."'"If no rhythm to store, hit ENTER   ",a$
2980 IF a$="" THEN  RETURN
2990 FOR z=1 TO LEN a$: FOR y=1 TO LEN x$
3000 IF a$(z)=x$(y) THEN  GO TO 3030
3010 NEXT y
3020 PRINT "Your RHYTHM STRING contains invalid to
kens."'"The valid tokens are"'"      ";x$: GO TO 29
70
3030 NEXT z
3040 INPUT "Enter name of rhythm.   ",b$
3050 LET no of rhythms=no of rhythms+1
3060 IF no of rhythms>max THEN  PRINT ''"Sorry, to
o many rhythms.": LET no of rhythms=no of rhythms-
1: PRINT ''"enter CONT to continue": STOP : RETURN

3070 LET r$=r$+a$
3080 LET i$(no of rhythms)=b$
3090 LET s(no of rhythms)=LEN a$
3100 RETURN : REM  end of SUBr ******************

3110 REM  get rhythm SUBr *************************
3120 INPUT "Enter name of rhythm wanted"'"or if no
thing wanted, hit ENTER",b$
3130 IF b$="" THEN  RETURN
3140 LET start=1
3150 FOR z=LEN b$+1 TO 15: LET b$=b$+" ": NEXT z
```

Listing continued next page

```
3160 FOR z=1 TO no of rhythms
3170 IF i$(z)=b$ THEN  LET wanted=z: GO TO 3260
3180 LET start=start+s(z)
3190 NEXT z
3200 CLS : PRINT b$,"   not found"'"***************
**************************************************
"
3210 PRINT "Full list of names stored is"''
3220 FOR z=1 TO no of rhythms
3230 PRINT i$(z),s(z);" notes long"
3240 NEXT z: PRINT
3250 GO TO 3120
3260 REM name found
3270 LET a$=r$(start TO start+s(wanted)-1)
3280 PRINT b$,"found"'a$: RETURN : REM end of get
rhythm SUBr **************************************

3290 REM replay rhythm SUBr **********************
3300 GO SUB 3120: REM get rhythm
3310 IF b$="" THEN  RETURN
3320 FOR z=1 TO LEN a$
3330 LET c$=a$(z): LET duration=CODE c$-48: IF c$>
="a" THEN  LET duration=duration-39
3340 BEEP 0.1*duration,0
3350 NEXT z
3360 RETURN : REM   end of replay rhythm SUBr ****
**************************************************


3370 REM  alter rhythm SUBr **********************
3380 LET x$="123456789abcdefg"
3390 GO SUB 3120: REM get rhythm
3400 IF b$="" THEN  RETURN
3410 INPUT "Enter string to be changed."'"If nothi
ng to change, hit ENTER",o$
3420 IF o$="" THEN  RETURN
3430 LET olen=LEN o$
```

```
3440 FOR z=start TO start+s(wanted)-olen
3450 LET w=z
3460 IF o$=r$(w TO w+olen-1) THEN  GO TO 3500: REM
 string found
3470 NEXT z
3480 PRINT o$'"not found"
3490 INPUT "string not found"'"Hit ENTER and try a
gain",q$: GO TO 3410
3500 INPUT "Enter fresh string"'"or hit ENTER to d
elete"'f$
3510 IF f$="" THEN  GO TO 3570
3520 FOR z=1 TO LEN f$: FOR y=1 TO LEN x$
3530 IF f$(z)=x$(y) THEN  GO TO 3560
3540 NEXT y
3550 PRINT "Your fresh string contains invalid tok
ens."'"The valid tokens are"'"      ";x$: GO TO 350
0
3560 NEXT z
3570 LET t$=r$(start+s(wanted) TO LEN r$): REM tai
l of unaltered rhythms stored after in r$
3580 LET h$=r$(start TO w-1)
3590 LET a$=h$+f$+r$(w+olen TO start+s(wanted)-1):
 PRINT ''"Rhythm is now"''a$
3600 LET r$=r$(1 TO start-1)+a$+t$
3610 LET s(wanted)=s(wanted)+LEN f$-olen: REM new
length of rhythm stored
3620 GO TO 3410
3630 RETURN : REM  end of alter rhythm SUBr ******
**************************************************
```

```
3640 REM ******     Rhythms Menu SUBr     *********
3650 LET x$="hsra STOP "
3660 CLS : PRINT '''TAB 9;"music program"';TAB 8;"
RHYTHMS  SUB-MENU"''
```

Listing continued next page

```
3670 PRINT "  choices available        token"'"  .
.................          ....."
3680 PRINT "  HELP (ie info)";TAB 29;"h"''
3690 PRINT "  STORE RHYTHM";TAB 29;"s"''
3700 PRINT "  REPLAY RHYTHM";TAB 29;"r"''
3710 PRINT "  ALTER RHYTHM";TAB 29;"a"''
3720 PRINT "  EXIT (return to Main Menu)";TAB 29;"
e"''
3730 PRINT "   STOP ";TAB 28;" STOP "
3740 INPUT "CHOOSE OPTION."'"Enter token",c$
3750 FOR z=1 TO LEN x$
3760 LET choice=z
3770 IF c$=x$(z) THEN  GO TO 3810
3780 NEXT z
3790 IF c$="e" THEN  RETURN
3800 INPUT "You entered """;CHR$ (CODE c$);""","'"
which is not in the menu."'"Try again",c$: GO TO 3
750
3810 GO SUB c(choice+r offset)
3820 GO TO 3650: REM  end of Rhythms Menu SUBr ***
**************************************************
```

```
3830 REM ********   Compose Menu SUBr     *********
3840 LET x$="hcp STOP ": REM    sequence of menu-c
hoice tokens
3850 CLS : PRINT '''TAB 9;"music program"';TAB 7;"
COMPOSE  SUB-MENU"''
3860 PRINT "Sub-menus available        token"'"...
.................          ....."
3870 PRINT "  HELP (ie info)";TAB 29;"h"''
3880 PRINT "  COMBINE RHYTHM & TUNE";TAB 29;"c"''
3890 PRINT "  PLAY OPUS";TAB 29;"p"''
3900 PRINT "  EXIT (return to Main Menu)";TAB 29;"
```

```
e"''
3910 PRINT "   STOP ";TAB 28;" STOP "
3920 INPUT "CHOOSE SUB-MENU."'"Enter token",c$
3930 FOR z=1 TO LEN x$
3940 LET choice=z
3950 IF c$=x$(z) THEN  GO TO 3990
3960 NEXT z
3970 IF c$="e" THEN  RETURN
3980 INPUT "You entered """;CHR$ (CODE c$);"""",''"
which is not in the menu."'"Try again",c$: GO TO 3
930
3990 GO SUB c(c offset+choice)
4000 GO TO 3840: REM   end of Compose Menu SUBr **
***********************************************



4010 REM combine rhythm & tune  SUBr *************
4020 PRINT "Rhythm ";: GO SUB 3120: REM get rhythm
4030 IF b$="" THEN  RETURN
4040 PRINT '"Combining with"'"tune ";
4050 LET d$=a$
4060 LET dlen=LEN d$
4070 GO SUB 1120: REM get tune
4080 IF b$="" THEN  RETURN
4100 LET alen=LEN a$
4110 GO SUB 4160: REM least common multiple (dlen,
 alen)
4120 PRINT '"This opus is ";lcm;" notes long."'"Pl
ease wait while the musical"'"score is being writt
en."
4130 GO SUB 4300: REM marry tune & rhythm, to prod
uce OPUS
4140 GO SUB 4450: REM play opus
4150 RETURN : REM ********************************
```

Listing continued next page

```
4160 REM lcm SUBr ********************************
4170 LET alen=LEN a$: LET dlen=LEN d$
4180 IF alen>dlen THEN  LET big=alen: LET small=dl
en: GO TO 4200
4190 LET big=dlen: LET small=alen
4200 LET rem=big-small*INT (big/small)
4210 IF rem=0 THEN  GO TO 4240
4220 LET big=small: LET small=rem
4230 GO TO 4200
4240 LET hcf=small
4250 LET a factor=dlen/hcf
4260 LET d factor=alen/hcf
4270 LET lcm=a factor*d factor*hcf
4280 RETURN : REM ********************************


4290 REM marry tune & rhythm SUBR ****************
4300 DIM u$(lcm)
4310 LET first=1: LET last=alen
4320 FOR z=1 TO a factor
4330 LET u$(first TO last)=a$
4340 LET first=first+alen
4350 LET last=last+alen
4360 NEXT z
4370 DIM v$(lcm)
4380 LET first=1: LET last=dlen
4390 FOR z=1 TO d factor
4400 LET v$(first TO last)=d$
4410 LET first=first+dlen
4420 LET last=last+dlen
4430 NEXT z
4440 RETURN : REM ********************************


4450 REM play opus SUBr **************************
4460 IF lcm=0 THEN  PRINT "No OPUS composed yet.":
 INPUT "press ENTER to continue";c$: RETURN
```

```
4470 FOR z=1 TO lcm
4480 LET c$=v$(z): LET duration=CODE c$-48: IF c$>
="a" THEN  LET duration=duration-39
4490 LET pitch=k(CODE u$(z))
4500 IF pitch=1000 THEN  PAUSE (5*duration): GO TO
 4520
4510 BEEP duration*0.1,pitch
4520 NEXT z
4530 RETURN : REM ***********************************


4540 REM  Variations Sub-Menu SUBr ***************
4550 LET x$="hrip STOP "
4560 CLS : PRINT '''TAB 9;"music program"';TAB 8;"
VARIATIONS  SUB-MENU"''
4570 PRINT "  choices available        token"'"  .
.................        ....."'
4580 PRINT "  HELP (ie info)";TAB 29;"h"''
4590 PRINT "  REVERSE";TAB 29;"r"''
4600 PRINT "  INVERT";TAB 29;"i"''
4610 PRINT "  PERMUTE";TAB 29;"p"''
4620 PRINT "  EXIT (return to Main Menu)";TAB 29;"
e"''
4630 PRINT "   STOP ";TAB 28;" STOP "
4640 INPUT "CHOOSE OPTION."'"Enter token",c$
4650 FOR z=1 TO LEN x$
4660 LET choice=z
4670 IF c$=x$(z) THEN  GO TO 4710
4680 NEXT z
4690 IF c$="e" THEN  RETURN
4700 INPUT "You entered """;CHR$ (CODE c$);""","'"
which is not in the menu."'"Try again",c$: GO TO 4
650
4710 GO SUB c(choice+v offset)
4720 GO TO 4550: REM end of Variations Menu SUBr *
*************************************************
```

Listing continued next page

```
4730 REM HELP subr ******************************
4740 RESTORE 4790: CLS
4750 FOR z=1 TO 13: READ f$: PRINT f$: IF f$="" TH
EN  RESTORE 4790: GO TO 4770
4760 NEXT z
4770 INPUT "For more, ENTER any letter"'"To return
 to MENU just hit ENTER"'c$: IF c$="" THEN  RETURN

4780 GO TO 4750
4790 DATA "       EVERYBODY'S  PLAYING"+CHR$ 13
4792 DATA "        THE MUSIC  PROGRAM"+CHR$ 13+CHR$
 13
4794 DATA "What Beethoven would have given"
4796 DATA "for this !!!"+CHR$ 13
4798 DATA "The MUSIC PROGRAM lets you"
4800 DATA "compose simple melodies. It"
4810 DATA "provides MENUs from which you"
4820 DATA "choose what to do."+CHR$ 13
4830 DATA "To enter a TUNE, YOU dont need"
4840 DATA "to be able to read music. Just"
4850 DATA "choose the PLAY KEYBOARD option,"
4860 DATA "play by ear the TUNE you want,"
4870 DATA "and write down the sequence of"
4880 DATA "'keytops' needed to play it."+CHR$ 13
4890 DATA "Then choose STORE TUNE and store"
4900 DATA "the sequence you wrote down."
4910 DATA "The sequence of notes for a TUNE"
4920 DATA "is entered, and stored, quite"
4930 DATA "separately from the sequence of"
4940 DATA "digits giving the length of each"
4950 DATA "note (the RHYTHM)."+CHR$ 13
4954 DATA "The SPACE token can be used to"
4956 DATA "indicate a silent pause."+CHR$ 13
4960 DATA "RHYTHMs are stored as strings of"
4970 DATA "digits (0 to 9), together with"
4984 DATA "the letters, ""a"" to ""g"", to"
4986 DATA "represent the values, 10 to 16."
```

```
4990 DATA "These values give the length of"
4994 DATA "each note or pause. A note or"
4996 DATA "pause of length 3 lasts about"
4998 DATA "one second."+CHR$ 13
5000 DATA "REPLAY TUNE gives you a replay"
5010 DATA "of any TUNE already stored, but"
5020 DATA "every note has the same length."+CHR$ 1
3
5030 DATA "REPLAY RHYTHM plays the rhythm,"
5040 DATA "but always uses the same note."+CHR$ 13
5050 DATA "To marry a TUNE to a RHYTHM, you"
5060 DATA "choose COMPOSE. This creates"
5070 DATA "and plays an OPUS (a musical"
5080 DATA "work!). You can always rehear"
5090 DATA "your last OPUS, by choosing"
5100 DATA "PLAY OPUS. Then you can hear the"
5104 DATA "tune & rhythm you have chosen,"
5106 DATA "played together, each note or"
5108 DATA "pause with its proper length."+CHR$ 13
5110 DATA "But the most interesting part"
5120 DATA "of the program is the VARIATIONS"
5130 DATA "Menu. The computer will turn a"
5140 DATA "TUNE 'upside-down', (INVERT it),"
5150 DATA "so that high notes become low,"
5160 DATA "and vice versa: it will turn a"
5170 DATA "TUNE back to front,(REVERSE it):"
5180 DATA "or it will PERMUTE a TUNE by"
5190 DATA "reversing the order of the notes"
5200 DATA "in each short group of up to 7"
5210 DATA "notes. Any of these VARIATIONS"
5220 DATA "may be stored as a new TUNE with"
5230 DATA "its own new name."+CHR$ 13
5240 DATA "If you choose REPLAY TUNE, and"
5250 DATA "ask for a TUNE whose name is not"
5260 DATA "stored, the computer tells you"
5270 DATA "so, and gives you a list of"
```

Listing continued next page

```
5280 DATA "TUNES it DOES have in store."+CHR$ 13
5290 DATA "As a starting bonus, the program"
5300 DATA "begins with several TUNES and"
5310 DATA "their corresponding RHYTHMs in"
5320 DATA "store already. So you might like"
5330 DATA "to begin by 'composing' ""When"
5340 DATA "Irish eyes are smiling"", by"
5350 DATA "choosing COMPOSE, and COMBINING"
5360 DATA "the RHYTHM and TUNE of"
5370 DATA """irisheyes""."+CHR$ 13
5380 DATA "You can even try combining a"
5390 DATA "TUNE with a strange RHYTHM !"
5400 DATA "Or try combining VARIATIONS of"
5410 DATA "a TUNE with its own RHYTHM, -"
5420 DATA "invert the tune of "
5430 DATA """irisheyes"" for a completely"
5440 DATA "new and appealing OPUS."+CHR$ 13
5450 DATA "PLAYING THE MICRO-HARPSICHORD. "
5460 DATA "Each digit or letter on the"
5470 DATA "keyboard will now produce a"
5480 DATA "trill of the notes in the major"
5490 DATA "chord for each note of the"
5500 DATA "scale. The lowest note is from"
5510 DATA "the ""1"" key, and the pitch goes"
5520 DATA "up by one half-tone at a time"
5530 DATA "as you move along the keyboard,"
5540 DATA "until the letter ""m"" is"
5550 DATA "reached."+CHR$ 13
5560 DATA "To continue with higher notes,"
5570 DATA "hold down the SYMBOL SHIFT key,"
5580 DATA "and start again at ""1""."
5590 DATA "Using SYMBOL SHIFT with any key"
5600 DATA "increases its pitch by exactly"
5610 DATA "three octaves. Each octave"
5620 DATA "contains 12 half-tones. This is"
5630 DATA "just what you have on a piano"
5640 DATA "keyboard (including white and"
```

```
5650 DATA "black keys). Middle C is the"
5660 DATA "letter ""o"""."+CHR$ 13
5670 DATA "When you want to stop playing"
5680 DATA "the micro-harpsichord, and go"
5690 DATA "back to the MAIN MENU, press"
5700 DATA "either the ENTER or SPACE key."+CHR$ 13
+CHR$ 13
5710 DATA "******************************"
5720 DATA "**  End of HELP information **"
5730 DATA "******************************"+CHR$ 13
+CHR$ 13
5740 DATA ""
5750 DATA ""
5760 REM end of HELP *****************************


6000 REM signature opus SUBr *********************
6010 LET e$="&))<=>=)&)>=($!$&$@!@!@$&()$<=<=)<=&)
)<=>=)&)>=($!$&$@!@n!v&'&$@!n!!"
6020 LET g$="2424228114242a11424226224242a24242281
14242a114242641122242a"
6030 LET sig=LEN g$: DIM u$(sig): DIM v$(sig)
6040 LET lcm=LEN e$: LET u$=e$: LET v$=g$
6050 GO SUB 4450: REM play opus
6060 RETURN : REM ********************************
6100 REM *************  T H E  E N D   ***********
**************************************************
```

4 ALPHABETIC INDEX OF KEYWORDS, CODES, AND KEYBOARD POSITIONS

Keyword	Code	position	Mode
ABS	189	on "g" key,	in E MODE.
ACS	182	on "w" key,	in E MODE.
ASN	181	on "q" key,	in E MODE.
ATN	183	on "e" key,	in E MODE.
ATTR	171	on "l" key,	in E MODE.
BEEP	215	on "z" key,	in E MODE.
BIN	196	on "b" key,	in E MODE.
BORDER	231	on "b" key,	in K MODE.
BRIGHT	220	on "b" key,	in E MODE.
CAT	207	on "9" key,	in E MODE.
CHR$	194	on "u" key,	in E MODE.
CIRCLE	216	on "h" key,	in E MODE.
CLEAR	253	on "x" key,	in K MODE.
CLOSE #	212	on "5" key,	in E MODE.
CLS	251	on "v" key,	in K MODE.
CODE	175	on "i" key,	in E MODE.
CONTINUE	232	on "c" key,	in K MODE.
COPY	255	on "z" key,	in K MODE.
COS	179	on "w" key,	in E MODE.
DATA	228	on "d" key,	in E MODE.
DEF FN	206	on "1" key,	in E MODE.
DIM	233	on "d" key,	in K MODE.
DRAW	252	on "w" key,	in K MODE.
ERASE	210	on "7" key,	in E MODE.
EXP	185	on "x" key,	in E MODE.
FLASH	219	on "v" key,	in E MODE.
FN	168	on "2" key,	in E MODE.
FOR	235	on "f" key,	in K MODE.
FORMAT	208	on "0" key,	in E MODE.
GO SUB	237	on "h" key,	in K MODE.
GO TO	236	on "g" key,	in K MODE.
IF	250	on "u" key,	in K MODE.
IN	191	on "i" key,	in E MODE.
INK	217	on "x" key,	in E MODE.
INKEY$	166	on "n" key,	in E MODE.
INPUT	238	on "i" key,	in K MODE.
INT	186	on "r" key,	in E MODE.
INVERSE	221	on "m" key,	in E MODE.
LEN	177	on "k" key,	in E MODE.

Keyword	Code	position	Mode
LET	241	on "l" key,	in K MODE.
LINE	202	on "3" key,	in E MODE.
LIST	240	on "k" key,	in K MODE.
LLIST	225	on "v" key,	in E MODE.
LN	184	on "z" key,	in E MODE.
LOAD	239	on "j" key,	in K MODE.
LPRINT	224	on "c" key,	in E MODE.
MERGE	213	on "t" key,	in E MODE.
MOVE	209	on "6" key,	in E MODE.
NEW	230	on "a" key,	in K MODE.
NEXT	243	on "n" key,	in K MODE.
OPEN #	211	on "4" key,	in E MODE.
OUT	223	on "o" key,	in E MODE.
OVER	222	on "n" key,	in E MODE.
PAPER	218	on "c" key,	in E MODE.
PAUSE	242	on "m" key,	in K MODE.
PEEK	190	on "o" key,	in E MODE.
PI	167	on "m" key,	in E MODE.
PLOT	246	on "q" key,	in K MODE.
POINT	169	on "8" key,	in E MODE.
POKE	244	on "o" key,	in K MODE.
PRINT	245	on "p" key,	in K MODE.
RANDOMIZE	249	on "t" key,	in K MODE.
READ	227	on "a" key,	in E MODE.
REM	234	on "e" key,	in K MODE.
RESTORE	229	on "s" key,	in E MODE.
RETURN	254	on "y" key,	in K MODE.
RND	165	on "t" key,	in E MODE.
RUN	247	on "r" key,	in K MODE.
SAVE	248	on "s" key,	in K MODE.
SCREEN$	170	on "k" key,	in E MODE.
SGN	188	on "f" key,	in E MODE.
SIN	178	on "q" key,	in E MODE.
SQR	187	on "h" key,	in E MODE.
STOP	226	on "a" key,	in K, L or C MODE.
STR$	193	on "y" key,	in E MODE.
TAB	173	on "p" key,	in E MODE.
TAN	180	on "e" key,	in E MODE.
USR	192	on "l" key,	in E MODE.
VAL	176	on "j" key,	in E MODE.
VAL$	174	on "j" key,	in E MODE.
VERIFY	214	on "r" key,	in E MODE.

Index of subroutines and programs

General Index